How to use this book

Matched to the National Curriculum, this Collin... Workbook is designed to improve mental maths skills.

Handy **tips** included throughout.

Questions split into three levels of difficulty – **Challenge 1**, **Challenge 2** and **Challenge 3** – to help progression.

Teaching notes to guide you through some of the key aspects of mental maths.

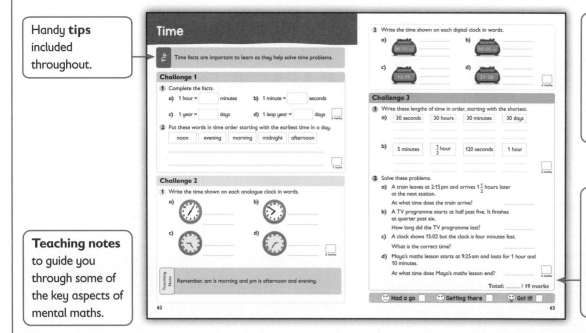

Total marks boxes for recording progress and 'How am I doing?' checks for self-evaluation.

Starter test recaps skills covered in Year 2.

Eight **audio tests** that can be accessed using the QR codes provided.

Four **Progress tests** included throughout the book for ongoing assessment and monitoring progress.

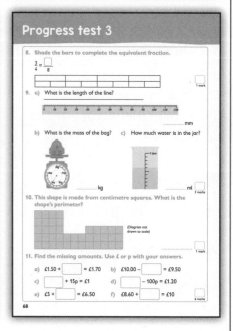

Answers provided for all the questions.

Contents

Acknowledgements

The authors and publisher are grateful to the copyright holders for permission to use quoted materials and images. All illustrations and images are ©Shutterstock.com and ©HarperCollins*Publishers* Ltd.

Published by Collins
An imprint of HarperCollins*Publishers*
1 London Bridge Street
London SE1 9GF

HarperCollins*Publishers*
Macken House, 39/40 Mayor Street Upper,
Dublin 1, D01 C9W8, Ireland

© HarperCollins*Publishers* Limited 2024

ISBN 978-0-00-867026-9

First published 2024

10 9 8 7 6 5 4 3 2 1

British Library Cataloguing in Publication Data.

A CIP record of this book is available from the British Library.

Publisher: Fiona McGlade
Authors: Sarah-Anne Fernandes and Trevor Dixon
Commissioning: Richard Toms
Editorial: Fiona Watson
Cover Design: Sarah Duxbury
Inside Concept Design and Page Layout: Ian Wrigley
Typesetting: Contentra Technologies (India)
Production: Bethany Brohm
Printed in the United Kingdom by Martins the Printers

MIX
Paper | Supporting
responsible forestry
FSC™ C007454

This book contains FSC™ certified paper and other controlled sources to ensure responsible forest management.

For more information visit: www.harpercollins.co.uk/green

Practising mental maths at home

Why is mental maths practice important?

Mental maths means being able to work out calculations in your head, without having to use a formal written method (though you can make jottings). During Key Stage 1 and Key Stage 2, children are taught mental maths strategies which help them to do this. These strategies also help them to develop a good sense of what numbers represent, and fluency in number facts such as pairs of numbers that add to 10 or 20, and multiplication tables.

By the end of Year 3, pupils are also expected to be able to "recall and use multiplication and division facts for the 3, 4 and 8 multiplication tables".

What you can do at home

Teach strategies to help your child complete calculations efficiently.

Strategy 1: Re-ordering and using number bonds

$3 + 30 + 17 =$
$17 + 3 = 20$
$30 + 20 = 50$

> Seeing the number bond to 20 of $17 + 3$ makes this calculation a combination of tens numbers.

Strategy 2: Partitioning

$2 \times 45 =$
$2 \times 40 = 80$
$2 \times 5 = 10$
$80 + 10 = 90$

> Partitioning 45 into 40 and 5 and doubling each, then re-combining the totals makes the calculation simpler.

Strategy 3: Compensating

$39 + 256 =$
$40 + 256 = 296$
$296 - 1 = 295$

> 39 is $40 - 1$
>
> Adding 40 to 256 is a much more straightforward calculation, but it's then necessary to make the adjustment by subtracting 1.

Strategy 4: Using place value

58 + 47 =

$$50 + 40 = 90$$
$$8 + 7 = 15$$
$$90 + 15 =$$

$$90 + 10 + 5$$
$$90 + 10 = 100$$
$$100 + 5 = 105$$

> Partitioning numbers, adding and re-combining reduces the issue of bridging a ten.

Making notes or jottings to help support mental calculations is quite acceptable; not everything needs to be held in the head, especially when working on calculations that involve more than one step.

Estimation: Estimation is a useful real-life skill. For example: How long will it take? Do I have enough money for these items? Estimating an answer to a calculation also helps your child check whether their answer to it is sensible. Practise estimating calculations, especially in real life, for instance when shopping or cooking.

Times tables: Being able to recall times tables really helps with mental maths. You can find singing games, rhymes and other activities on the internet to help your child learn their tables up to 12 × 12.

Time: With so many of us using phones and digital watches, many children find it difficult to tell the time from an analogue clock face. Practise telling the time, but also ask questions about timetables and TV programmes.

Measurements: In Years 3 and 4, children solve problems involving metric measures of length (mm, cm, km), mass (g and kg) and capacity (ml and L). They also begin to convert between some metric measures, for example kilograms to grams. Practical measuring, for example when cooking or doing DIY, will help your child.

Fractions: Help your child to develop an understanding of fractions as 'equal shares' and to be able to visualise different fractions; this will help them with fraction calculations. Ask your child to divide a cake or pizza into equal slices. What fraction is each slice? I eat two slices, what fraction is left?

Starter test

1. **Find one more than:**

   a) 15 ☐   b) 29 ☐

   Find one less than:

   c) 10 ☐   d) 16 ☐
   4 marks

2. **The arrows are pointing at numbers. What are the numbers?**

   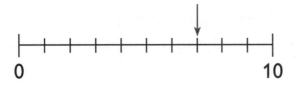   

   a) ....   b) ....
   2 marks

3. **Find the missing numbers.**

   a) $3 +$ ☐ $= 20$ b) ☐ $+ 16 = 18$

   c) $20 -$ ☐ $= 20$ d) ☐ $- 3 = 15$ ☐
   4 marks

4. **What fraction of each shape is shaded?**

   a) 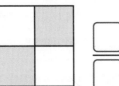   b) 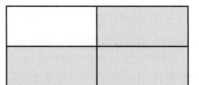
   2 marks

5. **These two 10 frames show two numbers.**

      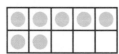

   Add the two numbers.   ....
   1 mark

6. **Circle all the squares.**

   1 mark

7. Here are some coins.

How much money is there altogether? ....

1 mark

8.

Chen has 12 cherries. He gives half of them to Sam.

How many cherries does he have left? ....

1 mark

9. Write these numbers in order, starting with the smallest.

   55   60   65   56

....

   Smallest

1 mark

10. Find the answers.

a) 34 + 4 = ☐   b) 87 − 5 = ☐

c) 92 − 60 = ☐   d) 26 + 30 = ☐

e) 15 + 16 = ☐   f) 6 + 3 + 4 = ☐

6 marks

11. Use <, > or = to compare these amounts.

a) £3 ◯ 300p   b) 3 metres ◯ 3 centimetres

c) 3 grams ◯ 3 kilograms   d) 3 minutes ◯ 3 hours

4 marks

12. Draw the shape that comes next in each sequence.

a)

b)

2 marks

13. a) Ben buys a pen for 50p and a rubber for 30p.

How much does he spend? ....

b) Toby buys a book for £5 and a comic for £3. He pays with a £10 note.

How much does he have left? ....

2 marks

14. Milly finds the answers to four problems.
Circle the answer she has got wrong.

$\frac{3}{4}$ of 4 = 3 $\frac{1}{3}$ of 9 = 3 $\frac{1}{2}$ of 10 = 4 $\frac{1}{4}$ of 16 = 4

1 mark

15. Omar counts in steps of three but he has missed some numbers.
Write the missing numbers.

3	6	9		15	18			27	30

1 mark

16. Find the answers.

a) $6 \times 5 = \boxed{}$

b) $12 \times 2 = \boxed{}$

c) $35 \div 5 = \boxed{}$

d) $18 \div 2 = \boxed{}$

e) $3 \times \boxed{} = 30$

f) $25 \div \boxed{} = 5$

6 marks

17. Beth makes a tally chart of the birds she sees in her back garden.

Bird	Tally
Blackbird	|||||	
Magpie	|||
Robin		
Sparrow	||||| ||||| |||

a)   How many birds does Beth see altogether?   ....

b)   How many more sparrows than magpies does Beth see?

....

2 marks

8

18. Zara builds a rocket using two shapes, as shown in the picture.
Circle the two shapes she uses.

    rectangle   cone   circle

        cylinder   pyramid

2 marks

19. This table shows the colour and size of some counters in a tub.

Colour \ Size	Small	Large
Blue	35	20
Red	25	15

a) How many red counters are there? ....

b) How many large counters are there? ....

2 marks

20. This shape is a square-based pyramid.

a) How many vertices are there? ....

b) How many edges are there? ....

c) How many faces are there? ....

3 marks

21. There are 100 cards in a set. Ari has 85 of the cards.
How many more of the cards does Ari need to
make a full set? ....

1 mark

22. A sack holds 20 kilograms of potatoes.
A cook uses half of the potatoes.
What mass of potatoes did the cook use? ....

1 mark

Total: _____ / 50 marks

Multiples

Challenge 1

1 Complete the number tracks with the missing multiples.

a) Multiples of 4

| 4 | | | 12 | 16 | | | | 28 | |

b) Multiples of 8

| 8 | | 24 | | 40 | | | 64 |

c) Multiples of 50

| 50 | 100 | | | 250 | 300 | | |

d) Multiples of 100

| 100 | 200 | 300 | 400 | | | | |

4 marks

2 Write the numbers 4, 8 and 50 on the flower pots to match the multiples shown on the flower petals.

a)

b)

c)

3 marks

Challenge 2

1 Sort the multiples into the correct place on the Venn diagram.

4   8   12   16   20   32   50   64

Multiples of 4   Multiples of 8

8 marks

2 Circle the odd one out in each set of multiples.

a)   200   400   500   650   700   800   100   900

b)   12   4   16   20   24   30   32   8

c)   50   100   200   150   225   250   300   700

d)   8   16   24   51   32   40   48   56

4 marks

Challenge 3

1 Which multiple of 8 is greater than 50 but less than 60? ....

1 mark

2 a)   Pat says, "Multiples of 50 are also multiples of 100"

Circle the correct statement:

Always true   Sometimes true   Never true

b)   Dev says, "Multiples of 100 are also multiples of 50"

Circle the correct statement:

Always true   Sometimes true   Never true

2 marks

3 Sam uses these digit cards to make multiples of 8 less than 100

2   6   8   4

List all the multiples Sam can make.   ....

1 mark

4 Mia says, "My favourite number is 100 because it is a multiple of 4, 8, 50 and 100"

Explain why Mia is incorrect. ....

....

1 mark

Total: _____ / 24 marks

 Had a go ☐    Getting there ☐   😄 Got it! ☐

Place value

Challenge 1

1 Write the represented numbers in numerals and words.

a)

Hundreds	Tens	Ones
100 100	10 10 10 10 10 10 10 10 10	1 1 1 1 1

Numeral: ....

Words: ....

b)

Hundreds	Tens	Ones
100 100 100	10 10 10 10 10	1 1 1

Numeral: ....

Words: ....

4 marks

2 Fill in the missing parts in these part-whole models.

a)
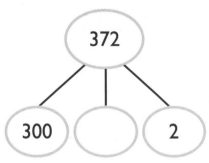

b)
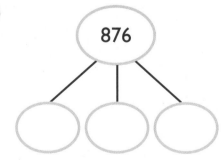

4 marks

12

Challenge 2

1 Fill in the missing numbers to make these calculations correct.

   a) 725 = 700 + 20 + [   ]

   b) 369 = 300 + [   ] + 9

   c) 912 = 900 + [   ] + 2

   d) 640 = 600 + 40 + [   ]   [   ] 4 marks

2 Label these ribbons from 1 to 5 from shortest to longest.

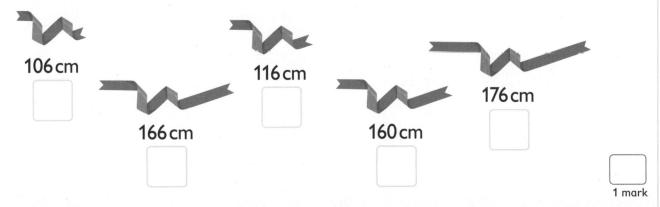

106 cm [   ]

116 cm [   ]

166 cm [   ]

160 cm [   ]

176 cm [   ]

[   ] 1 mark

Challenge 3

1 What numbers are shown by the arrows on this number line?

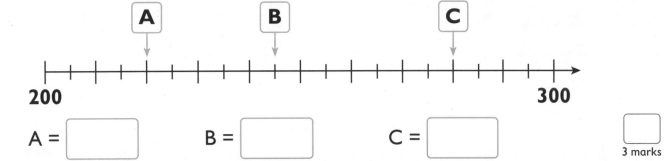

200   300

A = [   ]   B = [   ]   C = [   ]   [   ] 3 marks

2 Here are some numbers:

   552   524   422   245

Add them to this number track. The numbers are in order, starting with the smallest.

	254		424		544	

[   ] 4 marks

Total: _____ / 20 marks

 Had a go [   ]   **Getting there** [   ]   **Got it!** [   ]

Finding 10 or 100 more or less

Challenge 1

 1 Draw one extra counter on each place value chart to find the answer.

a)

Hundreds	Tens	Ones
100 100	10 10 10	1 1 1 1 1 1

10 more than 236 is ⬚

b)

Hundreds	Tens	Ones
100	10 10 10	1 1 1 1

100 more than 134 is ⬚

2 marks

 2 Cross off a bead on each abacus to find the answer.

a)

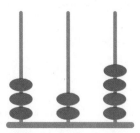

10 less than 324 is ⬚

b)

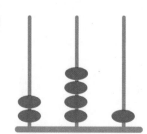

10 less than 241 is ⬚

2 marks

Challenge 2

1 Sam makes this number with ones (1) and rods (10). Complete the table for Sam's number.

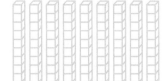

100 more	10 more	10 less
a)	b)	c)

3 marks

2 Complete the sentences.

a) 10 less than 918 is ....   b) 100 more than 526 is ....

c) 10 more than 598 is ....   d) 100 less than .... is 789

e) 100 more than 900 is ....   f) 10 less than .... is 655

6 marks

Challenge 3

1 Find the missing numbers to make these calculations correct.

a) $275 + \boxed{} = 285$

b) $754 - \boxed{} = 654$

c) $38 + \boxed{} = 138$

d) $917 - \boxed{} = 907$

e) $\boxed{} + 100 = 101$

f) $\boxed{} - 10 = 505$

 6 marks

2 A teacher has 24 pencils. There are new boxes of 10 pencils in the cupboard. She gets two boxes.

How many pencils will she have now? .... 1 mark

3 These 10 frames show a number.

10	10	10	10	10
10	10	10	10	10

10	10	10	10	10
10	10	10	10	10

10	10	10	10	10

Polly takes away one whole 10 **frame** and adds one more 10 **counter**.

What number will the 10 frames show now? .... 1 mark

4 Chen has a number with four hundreds, seven tens and six ones. He subtracts 10 from his number.

What is his new number? Write your answer in digits.

.... 1 mark

Total: _____ / 22 marks

 Had a go ☐   **Getting there** ☐   😄 **Got it!** ☐

15

Addition

Challenge 1

1 Complete the calculations, using the abacuses to help you.

a) Add 3 more ones beads to the abacus.

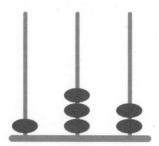

132 + 3 = ☐

b) Add 4 more tens beads to the abacus.

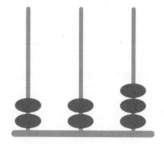

223 + 40 = ☐

c) Add 2 more hundreds beads to the abacus.

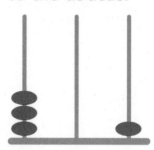

301 + 200 = ☐

d) Add 5 more ones beads to the abacus.

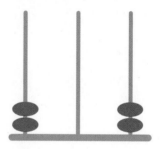

202 + 5 = ☐

☐ 4 marks

2 Work out the answers mentally.

a) 205 + 4 = ☐

b) 340 + 6 = ☐

c) 730 + 20 = ☐

d) 615 + 30 = ☐

☐ 4 marks

Challenge 2

1 Work out the answers mentally.

a) 585 + 8 = ☐

b) 260 + 90 = ☐

c) 495 + 20 = ☐

d) 421 + 200 = ☐

☐ 4 marks

2 Join the numbers that add to make 500

| 300 | 460 | 493 | 399 | 150 | 455 |

| 7 | 350 | 45 | 200 | 40 | 101 |

6 marks

Challenge 3

1 A survey was completed to find out how many children walk to school.

Complete the missing numbers in the table.

			Total
Key Stage 1	Year 1	Year 2	
	55	20	a) ....
Lower Key Stage 2	Year 3	Year 4	
	40	20	b) ....
Upper Key Stage 2	Year 5	Year 6	
	15	35	c) ....
Whole school			d) ....

4 marks

2 There are 265 pencils in a school.

The teacher buys another three packs of 100 pencils.

How many pencils does the school have altogether? ....

1 mark

3 Lily has walked 595 metres to school.

She sees a sign that says, 'School: 50 metres.'

How far will she have walked altogether when she reaches the school?

....

1 mark

Total: _____ / 24 marks

😐 Had a go ☐   🙂 Getting there ☐   😃 Got it! ☐

Subtraction

Challenge 1

1 Complete the calculations.

a) Take away 2 of the ones beads.

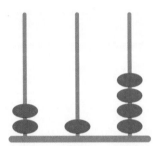

214 − 2 = ☐

b) Take away 2 of the tens beads.

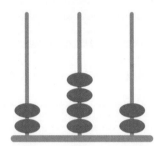

242 − 20 = ☐

c) Take away 4 of the ones beads.

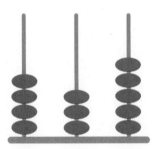

435 − 4 = ☐

d) Take away 3 of the hundreds beads.

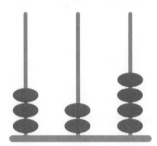

324 − 300 = ☐

☐ 4 marks

2 Work out the answers mentally.

a) 717 − 5 = ☐

b) 334 − 20 = ☐

c) 858 − 6 = ☐

d) 682 − 500 = ☐

☐ 4 marks

Challenge 2

1 Work out the answers mentally.

a) 345 − 6 = ☐

b) 254 − 8 = ☐

c) 725 − 30 = ☐

d) 308 − 10 = ☐

☐ 4 marks

2 Write <, > or = between these calculations to make each number statement correct.

a) 832 – 2 ◯ 840 – 20

b) 516 – 10 ◯ 525 – 8

c) 735 – 4 = ◯ 748 – 40

d) 205 – 20 = ◯ 194 – 9

4 marks

Challenge 3

1 Find the missing numbers.

a) 387 – ☐ = 384

b) ☐ – 5 = 422

c) 592 – ☐ = 522

d) ☐ – 700 = 84

4 marks

2 Find the number that is **1** hundred, **1** ten and **1** one less than **987**

....

1 mark

3 Hiran uses ones (1), rods (10) and flats (100) to show a number.

Hiran makes this number:

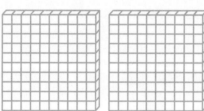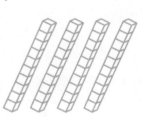

He takes away a flat, two rods and four ones.

What number is left? ....

1 mark

4 Pencils can be bought in boxes of 100 or in boxes of 10

A school has 370 pencils but needs 1000

What is the smallest number of boxes needed to make sure there are exactly 1000 pencils?

....

1 mark

Total: _____ / 23 marks

Multiplication: 3 times table

Challenge 1

1 Complete the sentences using the pictures to help you.

a)

There are .... groups of .... cupcakes.

There are .... cupcakes in total.

b)

There are .... groups of .... pencils.

There are .... pencils in total.

c)

There are .... groups of .... balls.

There are .... balls in total.

3 marks

2 Fill in the missing numbers in the times table grids.

a)

	× 3
1	
3	
7	
9	

b)

	× 3
2	
11	
4	
10	

c)

	× 3
8	
6	
12	
5	

3 marks

Challenge 2

1 Circle all the calculations that match the array.

3 + 3 + 3 + 3   4 × 3   12 – 3

4 + 4 + 4 + 4   12 + 4   3 × 4

3 marks

2 Join the multiplication fact to the corresponding division fact.

| 9 × 3 | 4 × 3 | 7 × 3 | 5 × 3 | 10 × 3 | 2 × 3 |

| 30 ÷ 3 | 21 ÷ 3 | 15 ÷ 3 | 27 ÷ 3 | 12 ÷ 3 | 6 ÷ 3 |

6 marks

3 Work out the missing numbers.

a) 3 × ☐ = 36

b) 30 = 3 × ☐

c) 8 × 3 = ☐

d) ☐ ÷ 3 = 7

4 marks

Challenge 3

1 Ted buys six packs of three apples.

How many apples does he buy altogether? ....

1 mark

2 Cans of juice are bought in packs of three. Mark has 27 cans.

How **many more** packs of three does Mark need to buy so he has 60 cans? ....

1 mark

3 Mia has three 5p coins and three 10p coins.

How much does she have altogether? ....

1 mark

4 Omar buys three packs of three pens.

How many pens does he have altogether? ....

1 mark

Total: _____ / 23 marks

 Had a go ☐   **Getting there** ☐   **Got it!** ☐

Multiplication: 4 times table

Challenge 1

1 Complete the sentences using the pictures to help you.

a)

There are .... groups of .... cans.

There are .... cans in total.

b)

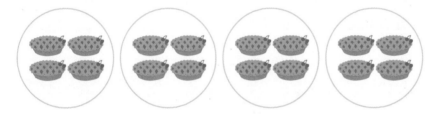

There are .... groups of .... pies.

There are .... pies in total.

c)

There are .... groups of .... flowers.

There are .... flowers in total.

3 marks

2 Fill in the missing numbers in the times table grids.

a)

	× 4
5	
2	
10	
3	

b)

	× 4
1	
4	
11	
8	

c)

	× 4
6	
7	
9	
12	

3 marks

Challenge 2

1 Circle all the calculations that match the array.

4 + 4 + 4 + 4   4 × 4   16 + 4

4 – 4 – 4 – 4   16 – 4   16 ÷ 4

3 marks

2 Join the multiplication fact to the corresponding division fact.

8 × 4	6 × 4	10 × 4	12 × 4	3 × 4	7 × 4

24 ÷ 4	32 ÷ 4	48 ÷ 4	40 ÷ 4	28 ÷ 4	12 ÷ 4

6 marks

3 Work out the missing numbers.

a) 4 × ☐ = 8

b) 32 = 4 × ☐

c) 4 × 4 = ☐

d) ☐ ÷ 4 = 6

e) 44 = ☐ × 4

f) ☐ = 20 ÷ 4

6 marks

Challenge 3

1 There are 12 stamps in a book of stamps.

How many stamps will be in four books? ....

1 mark

2 Oranges are bought in bags of four. Mark has 16 oranges.

How many **more bags** of four does Mark need
to buy so he has 48 oranges? ....

1 mark

3 Mo has four 20p coins and four £2 coins.

How much does he have altogether? ....

1 mark

4 Neo buys four packs of five pens and three packs of four pens.

How many pens does he have altogether? ....

1 mark

Total: _____ / 25 marks

 Had a go ☐   Getting there ☐   Got it! ☐

Multiplication: 8 times table

Challenge 1

1 Complete the sentences using the pictures to help you.

a)

There are .... groups of .... balloons.

There are .... balloons in total.

b)

There are .... groups of .... pencils.

There are .... pencils in total.

c)

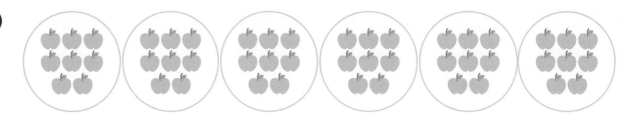

There are .... groups of .... apples.

There are .... apples in total.

3 marks

2 Fill in the missing numbers in the times table grids.

a)

	× 8
2	
11	
7	
4	

b)

	× 8
1	
9	
10	
3	

c)

	× 8
6	
8	
12	
5	

3 marks

Challenge 2

1 Join the multiplication fact to the corresponding division fact.

9 × 8	6 × 8	12 × 8	4 × 8	8 × 8	7 × 8

48 ÷ 8	32 ÷ 8	96 ÷ 8	72 ÷ 8	56 ÷ 8	64 ÷ 8

6 marks

2 Work out the missing numbers.

a) 8 × ☐ = 72

b) 56 = 8 × ☐

c) 8 × 3 = ☐

d) ☐ ÷ 8 = 8

e) 96 = ☐ × 8

f) ☐ = 8 ÷ 8

6 marks

Challenge 3

1 There are eight lights in every metre of fairy lights.

How many lights are in eight metres of fairy lights? ....

1 mark

2 There are eight footballers in a team. Twelve teams play in a competition.

How many footballers play in the competition? ....

1 mark

3 Mia and seven friends go to a burger bar. Each burger costs £5 and each drink costs £3.

If they all have a burger and a drink, how much does Mia spend? ....

1 mark

4 Max has three boxes of eight cards. He needs 40 cards.

How many **more boxes** does Max need so he has 40 cards altogether? ....

1 mark

Total: _____ / 22 marks

Progress test 1

1. **Use multiples of four to complete the number track.**

		12	16	20			32		40

1 mark

2. **Fill in the missing numbers in these part-whole models.**

a)

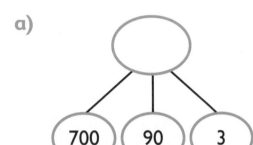

b)

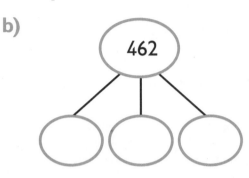

4 marks

3. **Work out the answers mentally.**

a) 426 + 3 = ☐   b) 759 − 40 = ☐

c) 241 + 500 = ☐   d) 876 − 300 = ☐

4 marks

4. **Complete this multiplication grid.**

×	3	a)	8
5	b)	20	c)
d)	e)	28	56

5 marks

5. a) Circle all the numbers that are **not** multiples of 50

   75   250   800   350   255   500   650   725

b) Circle all the numbers that are **not** multiples of 8

   24   32   48   54   60   16   38   64

6 marks

6. **Fill in the missing numbers to make these calculations correct.**

a) 367 = 300 + 60 + ☐   b) 832 = 800 + ☐ + 2

c) 904 = 900 + ☐ + 4   d) 517 = ☐ + 10 + 7

4 marks

7. **a)** Circle the longest length.

   105 cm   80 cm   230 cm   100 cm   99 cm

   b) Circle the heaviest mass.

   600 g   195 g   485 g   505 g   535 g

2 marks

8. **Complete the sentences.**

   a) 100 less than 365 is ....   **b)** 10 more than 708 is ....

   c) 10 more than 95 is ....   **d)** 100 less than .... is 176

4 marks

9. **Find the missing numbers.**

   a)   10 more   10 more

   [   ]   [494]   [   ]

   b)   100 less   100 less

   [   ]   [850]   [   ]

4 marks

10. Work out the answers mentally.

   a) 473 + 7 = [   ]   **b)** 440 + 80 = [   ]

   c) 299 + 200 = [   ]   **d)** 191 + 30 = [   ]

4 marks

11. Work out the answers mentally.

   a) 985 − 60 = [   ]   **b)** 777 − 7 = [   ]

   c) 284 − 200 = [   ]   **d)** 810 − 30 = [   ]

4 marks

27

Progress test 1

12. Work out the missing numbers.

a) $8 \times \boxed{} = 40$

b) $24 = 3 \times \boxed{}$

c) $12 \times 5 = \boxed{}$

d) $\boxed{} \div 8 = 4$

e) $48 = \boxed{} \times 8$

f) $\boxed{} = 60 \div 5$

$\boxed{}$ 6 marks

13. For each set of calculations, circle the calculation with a different answer.

a) $225 + 20 =$ $110 + 50 =$ $145 + 100 =$ $242 + 3 =$

b) $12 \times 2 =$ $6 \times 4 =$ $5 \times 5 =$ $3 \times 8 =$

c) $60 \div 10 =$ $35 \div 5 =$ $56 \div 8 =$ $28 \div 4 =$

$\boxed{}$ 3 marks

14. Sam uses these digit cards to make multiples of 4 less than 50

List all the multiples Sam can make. ....

$\boxed{}$ 1 mark

15. What numbers are shown by the arrows on this number line?

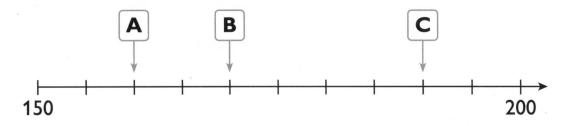

A = $\boxed{}$ B = $\boxed{}$ C = $\boxed{}$

$\boxed{}$ 3 marks

16. Anna has 23 muffin cases. There are new boxes of 100 muffin cases in the shop.

    She buys one new box.

    How many muffin cases will she have now? .... ☐ 1 mark

17. Mia has five 10p coins and two 20p coins.

    How much does she have altogether? .... ☐ 1 mark

18. There are eight crayons in a pack. A teacher uses 12 new packs for her class.

    How many crayons does she use altogether? .... ☐ 1 mark

19. A ferry can hold 150 foot passengers and 35 cars.

    There are 98 foot passengers and 21 cars on board.

    a) How many more foot passengers could the ferry carry? ....

    b) How many more cars could the ferry carry? .... ☐ 2 marks

20. Cans of drink are sold in packs of eight cans.

    Mason has 18 cans of drink, but needs 42

    How many more packs must he buy so he has enough cans? .... ☐ 1 mark

    Total: _____ / 61 marks

The questions for this test are found on the audio available on the QR code above. Listen to each question and write your answers in the spaces below. Try to answer the questions in the time allowed on the audio.

1. ....   **1 mark**

2. ....   **1 mark**

3. **21 ÷ 7**   **24 ÷ 4**   **28 ÷ 4**   **35 ÷ 7**   **1 mark**

4. a) ....   b) ....   **2 marks**

5. **4**   **12**   **15**   **20**   **24**   **30**   **2 marks**

6. ....   **1 mark**

7. **3** ▶   **400** ▶   **70** ▶   ....   **1 mark**

8. ....   **1 mark**

9. **80**   **115**   **140**   **200**   **205**   **1 mark**

10. ....   **1 mark**

Total: _____ / 12 marks

 Had a go ☐   **Getting there** ☐   **Got it!** ☐

Test Questions

The questions for this test are found on the audio available on the QR code above. Listen to each question and write your answers in the spaces below. Try to answer the questions in the time allowed on the audio.

1. ....

☐ 1 mark

2.

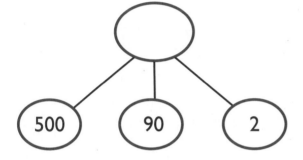

☐ 1 mark

3. 25   50   75   125   150

☐ 1 mark

4. a) ....   b) ....

☐ 2 marks

5.

☐ 1 mark

6. a) ....   b) ....

☐ 2 marks

7. $4 \times 3 = 2 \times \boxed{}$

☐ 1 mark

8. ....

☐ 1 mark

9. 648   642   462   862   846

☐ 1 mark

10. ....

☐ 1 mark

Total: _____ / 12 marks

 Had a go ☐   Getting there ☐   Got it! ☐

Multiplication: two-digit by one-digit numbers

Challenge 1

1 Complete the sentences.

a) 2 × 4 = 8 so 20 × 4 = ☐   b) 3 × 5 = 15 so 30 × 5 = ☐

c) 3 × 3 = 9 so 30 × 3 = ☐   d) 2 × 8 = 16 so 20 × 8 = ☐

e) 6 × 4 = 24 so 60 × 4 = ☐   f) 7 × 5 = 35 so 70 × 5 = ☐

☐ 6 marks

2 Use the bar models to complete the multiplications.

a) 18 × 5 = ☐

10 × 5	8 × 5

b) 14 × 3 = ☐

10 × 3	4 × 3

c) 23 × 4 = ☐

20 × 4	3 × 4

d) 62 × 2 = ☐

60 × 2	2 × 2

e) 38 × 2 = ☐

30 × 2	8 × 2

f) 43 × 4 = ☐

40 × 4	3 × 4

☐ 6 marks

Challenge 2

1 Complete the tables.

a)

1 box	5 boxes	10 boxes	12 boxes	15 boxes	20 boxes
3 eggs	☐ eggs	☐ eggs	☐ eggs	☐ eggs	☐ eggs

b)

1 pack	5 packs	10 packs	12 packs	15 packs	20 packs
4 pens	☐ pens	☐ pens	☐ pens	☐ pens	☐ pens

☐ 10 marks

2 Multiply these numbers.

a) 26 × 3 = ☐

b) 33 × 4 = ☐

c) 61 × 5 = ☐

d) 14 × 8 = ☐

e) 82 × 4 = ☐

f) 76 × 2 = ☐

☐ 6 marks

Challenge 3

1 A shop sells books for £4 each, pencils for £2 each and pens for £3 each.

Each class orders some items. Find the total cost for each class.

a) Class 3L has ordered 21 books and 10 pencils.

Total cost =   £ ....

b) Class 3M has ordered 13 books and 20 pens.

Total cost =   £ ....

c) Class 3T has ordered 12 books, 15 pencils and 10 pens.

Total cost =   £ ....   ☐ 3 marks

2 Solve these problems.

a) One sweet costs 8p. A bag has 24 sweets.

How much does the bag of sweets cost?   ....p

b) A length of string is cut into four pieces.
Each piece is 55 centimetres long.

How long was the length of string?   ....cm

c) A sack of potatoes has a mass of 35 kilograms.

What is the mass of five sacks of potatoes?   ....kg   ☐ 3 marks

Total: _____ / 34 marks

 Had a go ☐   **Getting there** ☐   😄 **Got it!** ☐

33

Multiplication and division problems

Challenge 1

1 Complete the multiplication grids.

a)

×	4	5	8
5	20		
	28		56
		8	10

b)

×		3	
6	24		
3		9	15
8			

14 marks

2 Write <, > or = between these calculations to make each number statement correct.

a) 4 × 8 ◯ 3 × 7

b) 36 ÷ 3 ◯ 4 x 3

c) 8 × 8 ◯ 4 × 12

d) 4 × 2 ◯ 96 ÷ 8

4 marks

Challenge 2

1 Complete these word problems.

a)   18 children are put in groups of three for a school trip.

How many groups will there be? ....

b)   There are 32 prizes to share across four classes.

How many prizes will each class receive? ....

2 marks

2 Switch numbers around in these multiplications to make them easier to solve. Part of the first one is done for you.

a) 3 × 12 × 2 = 3 × 2 × 12 = 6 × 12 = ☐

b) 2 × 12 × 4 = ☐ × ☐ × 12 = ☐ × 12 = ☐

c) 3 × 15 × 2 = ☐ × ☐ × 15 = ☐ × 15 = ☐

9 marks

Challenge 3

1 Find the missing numbers.

  a) $23 \times 4 = 20 \times \boxed{} + \boxed{} \times 4 = 80 + \boxed{} = 92$

  b) $42 \times 3 = \boxed{} \times 3 + 2 \times \boxed{} = 120 + \boxed{} = 126$ $\boxed{}$ 6 marks

2 Solve these problems.

  a) A sack of potatoes has a mass of 24 kilograms. A café owner buys three sacks.

    What is the mass of potatoes she has bought? .... kg

  b) A can of drink costs 72p. Kylie buys five cans.

    How much does Kylie spend? ....

  c) A gardener buys five packs of bulbs. There are 15 bulbs in each pack.

    How many bulbs does he buy? .... $\boxed{}$ 3 marks

3 Find the missing number in each multiplication.

  a) $\boxed{} \times 5 = 90$ **b)** $\boxed{} \times 4 = 60$

  c) $\boxed{} \times 3 = 39$ **d)** $\boxed{} \times 10 = 150$ $\boxed{}$ 4 marks

4 Find the missing digit in these multiplications.

  a) $2\boxed{} \times 3 = 60$ **b)** $\boxed{}0 \times 4 = 80$

  c) $\boxed{}0 \times 5 = 150$ **d)** $\boxed{}2 \times 4 = 128$ $\boxed{}$ 4 marks

5 There are eight cakes in a box. There are five boxes in a pack. Ms Singh buys five packs.

  How many cakes does she buy? .... cakes $\boxed{}$ 1 mark

Total: _____ **/ 47 marks**

 😐 **Had a go** ☐   🙂 **Getting there** ☐   😃 **Got it!** ☐

Tenths

Challenge 1

1 Match each shape to the correct fraction.

a) 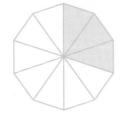 b)  c) 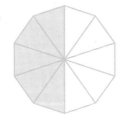 d)

$\frac{1}{10}$ $\frac{8}{10}$ $\frac{5}{10}$ $\frac{3}{10}$

4 marks

2 Show the correct fraction.

a) Colour $\frac{4}{10}$ of the rectangle.

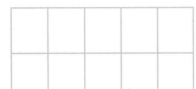

b) Colour $\frac{10}{10}$ of the rectangle.

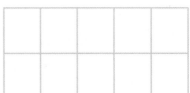

2 marks

Challenge 2

1 Write the fraction shown by the arrow on each number line.

a)

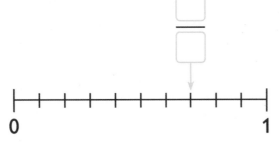

b)

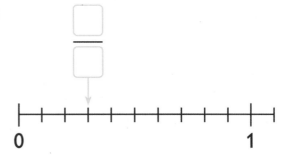

c)

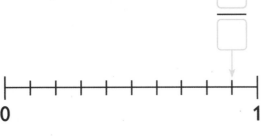

d)

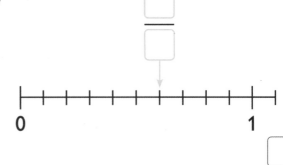

4 marks

When you divide by 10, each digit moves one place to the right.

2 Use the place value chart to help you divide by 10 and record your answer.

		Tens	Ones	.	tenths		Tens	Ones	.	tenths
a)	40 ÷ 10 =	4	0	.	0	÷ 10 =			.	
b)	20 ÷ 10 =	2	0	.	0	÷ 10 =			.	
c)	8 ÷ 10 =		8	.	0	÷ 10 =			.	

3 marks

Challenge 3

1 These tenths are in order, starting with the smallest.
Write the missing tenths.

$\frac{3}{10}$	—	$\frac{5}{10}$	—	—	$\frac{8}{10}$	—

4 marks

2 Use the place value chart to help you divide by 10 and record your answer.

		Tens	Ones	.	tenths		Tens	Ones	.	tenths
a)	36 ÷ 10 =	3	6	.	0	÷ 10 =			.	
b)	18 ÷ 10 =	1	8	.	0	÷ 10 =			.	
c)	94 ÷ 10 =	9	4	.	0	÷ 10 =			.	

3 marks

3 Write the missing number.

a) $\boxed{}$ ÷ 10 = $\frac{2}{10}$

b) $\boxed{}$ ÷ 10 = 4.9

2 marks

Total: _____ / 22 marks

 Had a go ☐   Getting there ☐   😄 Got it! ☐

Finding a fraction of a number

Teaching Note Use a bar model to divide a whole amount into fractional parts.

Challenge 1

1 Find a fraction of each set of marbles.

a) $\frac{1}{3}$ of 6 marbles = ☐

b) $\frac{1}{4}$ of 12 marbles = ☐

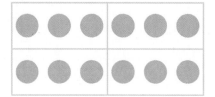

c) $\frac{1}{2}$ of 14 marbles = ☐

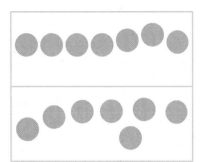

d) $\frac{1}{5}$ of 10 marbles = ☐

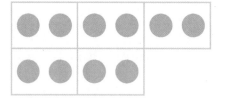

☐
4 marks

2 Use the bar model to find the fraction of each number.

a) $\frac{1}{3}$ of 12 = ☐

b) $\frac{1}{5}$ of 20 = ☐

☐
2 marks

38

Challenge 2

1. Complete the calculations using the bar model.

56							
7	7	7	7	7	7	7	7

a) $\frac{1}{8}$ of 56 = ☐

b) $\frac{2}{8}$ of 56 = ☐

c) $\frac{☐}{8}$ of 56 = 28

d) $\frac{5}{8}$ of 56 = ☐

e) $\frac{3}{8}$ of ☐ = 21

f) $\frac{☐}{8}$ of 56 = 56

6 marks

Challenge 3

1. Solve these problems.

a) How much more is $\frac{1}{2}$ of £16 than $\frac{1}{4}$ of £20? ....

b) How much more is $\frac{3}{4}$ of £12 than $\frac{2}{3}$ of £9? ....

2 marks

2. Solve these problems.

a) Alia has 20 felt tips. She gives $\frac{1}{4}$ of them to Milly.

How many felt tips does she have left? ....

b) Sally buys a bag of apples. She puts half of them in a bowl. Seven apples are left in the bag.

How many apples are in the bowl? ....

c) On a bus, $\frac{1}{3}$ of the passengers are children.

The rest are adults. There are 12 adults.

How many passengers are on the bus? ....

3 marks

Total: _____ / 17 marks

 Had a go ☐   Getting there ☐   Got it! ☐

39

Equivalent fractions

Tip

A fraction wall breaks down a whole into different fractions. You can use the wall to find equivalent fractions, e.g. $\frac{1}{2} = \frac{2}{4}$

1 Whole											
$\frac{1}{2}$						$\frac{1}{2}$					
$\frac{1}{3}$				$\frac{1}{3}$				$\frac{1}{3}$			
$\frac{1}{4}$			$\frac{1}{4}$			$\frac{1}{4}$			$\frac{1}{4}$		
$\frac{1}{5}$		$\frac{1}{5}$		$\frac{1}{5}$		$\frac{1}{5}$		$\frac{1}{5}$			
$\frac{1}{6}$		$\frac{1}{6}$		$\frac{1}{6}$		$\frac{1}{6}$		$\frac{1}{6}$		$\frac{1}{6}$	
$\frac{1}{7}$	$\frac{1}{7}$		$\frac{1}{7}$		$\frac{1}{7}$		$\frac{1}{7}$		$\frac{1}{7}$		$\frac{1}{7}$
$\frac{1}{8}$	$\frac{1}{8}$	$\frac{1}{8}$	$\frac{1}{8}$	$\frac{1}{8}$	$\frac{1}{8}$	$\frac{1}{8}$	$\frac{1}{8}$				
$\frac{1}{10}$	$\frac{1}{10}$	$\frac{1}{10}$	$\frac{1}{10}$	$\frac{1}{10}$	$\frac{1}{10}$	$\frac{1}{10}$	$\frac{1}{10}$	$\frac{1}{10}$	$\frac{1}{10}$		
$\frac{1}{12}$	$\frac{1}{12}$	$\frac{1}{12}$	$\frac{1}{12}$	$\frac{1}{12}$	$\frac{1}{12}$	$\frac{1}{12}$	$\frac{1}{12}$	$\frac{1}{12}$	$\frac{1}{12}$	$\frac{1}{12}$	$\frac{1}{12}$

Challenge 1

1 Use the fraction wall above to help you complete the statements.

a) $\frac{1}{2} = \frac{\square}{4}$

b) $\frac{1}{3} = \frac{\square}{6}$

c) $\frac{2}{8} = \frac{\square}{4}$

d) $\frac{1}{2} = \frac{\square}{8}$

e) $\frac{4}{6} = \frac{2}{\square}$

f) $\frac{3}{4} = \frac{6}{\square}$

6 marks

Challenge 2

1 Complete the table by putting a tick in the correct column to indicate whether the statements are True (T) or False (F). Use the fraction wall to help you.

	T	F		T	F
a) $\frac{1}{2}$ is equal to $\frac{1}{3}$			b) $\frac{2}{4}$ are equal to $\frac{4}{8}$		
c) $\frac{1}{3}$ is equal to $\frac{2}{6}$			d) $\frac{2}{7}$ are equal to $\frac{1}{4}$		
e) $\frac{3}{6}$ are equal to $\frac{1}{2}$			f) $\frac{7}{7}$ are equal to 1 whole		

6 marks

40

2 Shade in the bars and complete the equivalent fractions.

a) $\dfrac{2}{5} = \dfrac{\boxed{}}{10}$

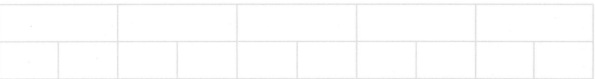

b) $\dfrac{2}{3} = \dfrac{\boxed{}}{12}$

2 marks

Challenge 3

1 Use <, > or = to compare each pair of fractions.

a) $\dfrac{2}{6} \bigcirc \dfrac{5}{6}$ b) $\dfrac{1}{2} \bigcirc \dfrac{2}{4}$ c) $\dfrac{8}{10} \bigcirc \dfrac{1}{5}$

3 marks

2 Shade each shape by the fraction shown.

a) Shade one half.

b) Shade three-quarters.

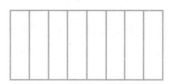

c) Shade two-fifths.

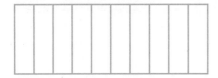

d) Shade two-thirds.

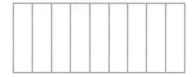

4 marks

3 Circle the two fractions that are equivalent.

$\dfrac{2}{3}$ $\dfrac{6}{8}$ $\dfrac{4}{5}$ $\dfrac{1}{2}$ $\dfrac{8}{10}$

1 mark

Total: _____ / 22 marks

 Had a go ☐   😊 **Getting there** ☐   😄 **Got it!** ☐

Adding and subtracting fractions

Teaching Note When adding or subtracting fractions with the same denominator, only add or subtract the numerator.

Challenge 1

1 Colour the shapes to add the fractions.

a) $\frac{1}{4} + \frac{2}{4} = \frac{\square}{4}$

b) $\frac{2}{5} + \frac{2}{5} = \frac{\square}{5}$

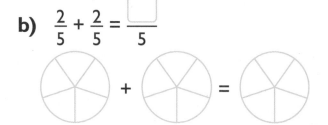

2 marks

2 Use the bars to work out these subtractions.

a) $\frac{3}{5} - \frac{1}{5} = \frac{\square}{5}$

b) $\frac{5}{6} - \frac{2}{6} = \frac{\square}{6}$

2 marks

Challenge 2

1 Calculate these additions and subtractions.

a) $\frac{3}{8} + \frac{1}{8} = \frac{\square}{\square}$

b) $\frac{4}{5} + \frac{2}{5} = \frac{\square}{\square}$

c) $\frac{1}{10} + \frac{6}{10} = \frac{\square}{\square}$

d) $\frac{7}{7} - \frac{1}{7} = \frac{\square}{\square}$

e) $\frac{4}{6} - \frac{3}{6} = \frac{\square}{\square}$

f) $\frac{7}{10} + \frac{2}{10} = \frac{\square}{\square}$

6 marks

2 Find the missing fraction.

a) $\frac{4}{8} + \frac{\square}{\square} = \frac{7}{8}$

b) $\frac{5}{6} - \frac{\square}{\square} = \frac{3}{6}$

c) $\frac{\square}{\square} + \frac{1}{10} = \frac{8}{10}$

d) $\frac{\square}{\square} - \frac{1}{3} = \frac{1}{3}$

4 marks

3 Write the addition and the answer shown by these shapes.

a)

$$ + \quad = \frac{\square}{\square} + \frac{\square}{\square} = \frac{\square}{\square} $$

b)

$$ + \quad = \frac{\square}{\square} + \frac{\square}{\square} = \frac{\square}{\square} $$

2 marks

Challenge 3

1 Work out the answers to these calculations.

a) $\frac{2}{8} + \frac{3}{8} + \frac{3}{8} = \frac{\square}{\square}$

b) $\frac{3}{10} + \frac{1}{10} + \frac{5}{10} = \frac{\square}{\square}$

c) $\frac{3}{9} + \frac{2}{9} + \frac{3}{9} = \frac{\square}{\square}$

d) $\frac{5}{12} + \frac{3}{12} + \frac{2}{12} = \frac{\square}{\square}$

4 marks

2 Solve these problems.

a) Leo has a bag of flour. It is $\frac{5}{8}$ full. He uses another $\frac{2}{8}$ of the bag.

What fraction of the bag is left now? ....

b) Jay uses $\frac{2}{5}$ of a tin of paint before lunch and another $\frac{2}{5}$ of the tin after lunch.

What fraction of the tin is left? ....

2 marks

3 Find the missing fraction in these calculations.

a) $\frac{5}{6} - \frac{3}{6} + \frac{\square}{\square} = \frac{4}{6}$

b) $\frac{2}{8} + \frac{\square}{\square} - \frac{4}{8} = \frac{5}{8}$

c) $\frac{\square}{\square} - \frac{5}{12} + \frac{1}{12} = \frac{3}{12}$

d) $\frac{5}{12} + \frac{\square}{\square} + \frac{2}{12} = \frac{11}{12}$

4 marks

Total: _____ / 26 marks

Comparing and ordering fractions

Challenge 1

1 Shade the fraction bars and then complete the sentences using the words **greater** and **smaller**.

a) $\frac{1}{4}$ is .... than $\frac{2}{4}$

b) $\frac{4}{5}$ is .... than $\frac{2}{5}$

c) $\frac{5}{10}$ is .... than $\frac{3}{10}$

d) $\frac{3}{8}$ is .... than $\frac{7}{8}$

4 marks

2 Compare the fractions. Write the larger fraction in each fraction pair.

a)

b)

c)

d)

4 marks

44

Challenge 2

1 Use the symbols <, > or = to compare the fractions.

a) $\frac{1}{6}$ ◯ $\frac{4}{6}$

b) $\frac{1}{2}$ ◯ $\frac{3}{6}$

c) $\frac{2}{3}$ ◯ $\frac{1}{3}$

d) $\frac{2}{8}$ ◯ $\frac{1}{8}$

4 marks

2 Order these fractions from largest to smallest.

a) $\frac{3}{5}$ $\frac{4}{5}$ $\frac{2}{5}$ $\frac{1}{5}$ ....

b) $\frac{6}{10}$ $\frac{3}{10}$ $\frac{2}{10}$ $\frac{8}{10}$ ....

c) $\frac{5}{6}$ $\frac{2}{6}$ $\frac{1}{6}$ $\frac{4}{6}$ ....

d) $\frac{7}{8}$ $\frac{3}{8}$ $\frac{8}{8}$ $\frac{5}{8}$ ....

4 marks

Challenge 3

1 Order these fractions from largest to smallest.

a) $\frac{1}{10}$ $\frac{1}{3}$ $\frac{1}{5}$ $\frac{1}{4}$ ....

b) $\frac{1}{8}$ $\frac{1}{6}$ $\frac{1}{12}$ $\frac{1}{10}$ ....

2 marks

2 Three fractions are written in order, starting with the smallest. One fraction is missing.

Circle the fraction that could be missing.

a) $\frac{3}{8}$ ☐ $\frac{7}{8}$ ☐ $\frac{6}{8}$ $\frac{1}{8}$ $\frac{7}{8}$ $\frac{8}{8}$

b) $\frac{1}{9}$ ☐ $\frac{1}{5}$ ☐ $\frac{1}{4}$ $\frac{1}{10}$ $\frac{1}{8}$ $\frac{1}{2}$

2 marks

Total: _____ / 20 marks

Progress test 2

1. Fill in the missing numbers in these multiplication grids.

    a)

×	4
4	
6	
9	
12	

    b)

×	8
3	
5	
8	
9	

    8 marks

2. Work out the answers mentally.

    a) $316 - 5 =$ [ ]

    b) $558 + 2 =$ [ ]

    c) $479 - 40 =$ [ ]

    d) $937 - 400 =$ [ ]

    4 marks

3. Circle the number that does not belong in each set of multiples.

    a) Multiples of 3

    9   36   24   18   29   15   12   21

    b) Multiples of 8

    96   88   24   48   56   36   16   64

    2 marks

4. Complete the sentences.

    a) 10 less than 518 is ....

    b) 100 more than 222 is ....

    c) 10 more than 465 is ....

    d) 100 less than 648 is ....

    4 marks

5. Circle all the numbers with a digit 4 with the value of four tens.

    124   348   412   414   841

    2 marks

6. Write <, > or = between these calculations to make each number statement correct.

   a) 5×6 ◯ 9×3 b) $36 \div 3$ ◯ 12×4

   c) $48 \div 4$ ◯ 5×2 d) $48 \div 8$ ◯ $36 \div 6$ ▢

   4 marks

7. Use the bar model to the find the fraction of each number.

   a) $\frac{1}{5}$ of 15 = ▢   b) $\frac{3}{4}$ of 16 = ▢

   ▢

   2 marks

8. Colour the shapes and add the fractions.

   a) $\frac{2}{4} + \frac{1}{4} = \frac{▢}{4}$ b) $\frac{3}{8} + \frac{2}{8} = \frac{▢}{8}$

   +   +

   ▢

   2 marks

9. Shade the fraction bars and then complete the sentences using the words 'greater' and 'smaller'.

   a) $\frac{3}{4}$ is .... than $\frac{1}{4}$ b) $\frac{1}{6}$ is .... than $\frac{5}{6}$

   ▢

   2 marks

10. Use the bar models to complete the multiplications.

   a) $17 \times 3 =$ ▢   b) $27 \times 5 =$ ▢

10×3	7×3

20×5	7×5

   ▢

   2 marks

11. Order these fractions from largest to smallest.

a) $\frac{3}{5}$ $\frac{1}{5}$ $\frac{4}{5}$ $\frac{2}{5}$ ....

b) $\frac{3}{8}$ $\frac{7}{8}$ $\frac{2}{8}$ $\frac{5}{8}$ ....

2 marks

12. A shop sells apples for 30p each and oranges for 40p each.

Find the total cost of:

a) 3 apples and 2 oranges   Total cost = ...

b) 5 apples and 2 oranges   Total cost = ...

c) 4 apples and 4 oranges   Total cost = ...

3 marks

13. Here are 12 stars:

How many is:

a) $\frac{1}{3}$ of the stars? .... b) $\frac{1}{4}$ of the stars? ....

c) $\frac{5}{12}$ of the stars? .... d) $\frac{5}{6}$ of the stars? ....

4 marks

14. Solve these problems.

a) A train has five coaches. There are 54 people in each coach.

How many people are on the train?

b) A school has 75 tickets for each show. There are three shows altogether.

How many tickets are there?

2 marks

15. Work out the answers to these calculations.

a) $\dfrac{1}{5} + \dfrac{2}{5} + \dfrac{1}{5} = \dfrac{\square}{\square}$

b) $\dfrac{3}{8} + \dfrac{1}{8} + \dfrac{3}{8} = \dfrac{\square}{\square}$

$\square$ 2 marks

16. Find the missing fraction in these calculations.

a) $\dfrac{9}{10} - \dfrac{8}{10} + \dfrac{\square}{\square} = \dfrac{2}{10}$

b) $\dfrac{3}{6} + \dfrac{\square}{\square} - \dfrac{4}{6} = \dfrac{1}{6}$

$\square$ 2 marks

17. Use < or > to compare each pair of fractions.

a) $\dfrac{7}{10} \bigcirc \dfrac{8}{10}$

b) $\dfrac{4}{8} \bigcirc \dfrac{1}{8}$

$\square$ 2 marks

18. Multiply these numbers.

a) $14 \times 8 = \boxed{}$

b) $45 \times 5 = \boxed{}$

c) $29 \times 3 = \boxed{}$

d) $34 \times 4 = \boxed{}$

$\square$ 4 marks

19. Solve these problems.

a) Nisha has 40 cans of drink. She gives $\dfrac{1}{8}$ of them to Sonya.

How many cans of drink does she have left? $\square$

b) Marty has a box of 100 pencils. He leaves 50 of them in the box. He gives half of the rest to other children.

How many pencils does he give to the other children? $\square$

$\square$ 2 marks

20. Write the missing number.

a) $\boxed{} \div 10 = \dfrac{7}{10}$

b) $\boxed{} \div 10 = 2.3$

$\square$ 2 marks

Total: _____ / 57 marks

The questions for this test are found on the audio available on the QR code above. Listen to each question and write your answers in the spaces below. Try to answer the questions in the time allowed on the audio.

1.

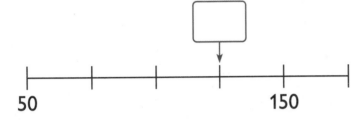

50   150

☐ 1 mark

2. ....

☐ 1 mark

3. ....

☐ 1 mark

4. ....

☐ 1 mark

5.

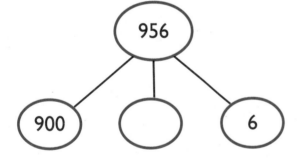

☐ 1 mark

6. a) ....   b) ....

☐ 2 marks

7. ....

☐ 1 mark

8. ....

☐ 1 mark

9. $\dfrac{1}{5}$ $\dfrac{1}{10}$ $\dfrac{1}{3}$

☐ 1 mark

10. a) ....   b) ....

☐ 2 marks

Total: _____ / 12 marks

 Had a go ☐   Getting there ☐   Got it! ☐

Audio test 4

The questions for this test are found on the audio available on the QR code above. Listen to each question and write your answers in the spaces below. Try to answer the questions in the time allowed on the audio.

1. ....

1 mark

2.

....

1 mark

3.   <   >   =

$\frac{4}{8}$ ◯ $\frac{6}{8}$

1 mark

4.   5 hundreds 9 ones 4 tens ....

1 mark

5.   480g   408g   485g   580g   584g

2 marks

6.   .... p

1 mark

7.   a) ....   b) ....

2 marks

8.   ....

1 mark

9. $\frac{2}{5}$ of 10   ....

1 mark

10.   ....

1 mark

Total: _____ / 12 marks

 Had a go ☐   Getting there ☐   😃 Got it! ☐

Length

Challenge 1

1. Circle the better estimate for each item.

a)

   2 m   **19 cm**

b)

   30 cm   **5 m**

c)

   20 cm   **2 m**

d)

   100 mm   **2 cm**

[ ] 4 marks

2. Read the scale on the ruler to complete the sentence.

a)

   The length of the pencil is

   .... cm.

b)

   The length of the pencil is

   .... cm.

[ ] 2 marks

Challenge 2

1. Complete these calculations.

   a) 150 cm + 30 cm = [   ] cm

   b) 300 cm + 80 cm = [   ] cm

   c) [   ] cm = 600 cm – 50 cm

   d) 900 cm – 150 cm = [   ] cm

   e) 450 cm + [   ] cm = 750 cm

   f) [   ] cm – 600 cm = 200 cm

[ ] 6 marks

Tip

Remember:

10 millimetres (mm) = 1 centimetre (cm)

100 centimetres (cm) = 1 metre (m)

2 Order these lengths from greatest to smallest.

a) 150 cm   105 cm   155 cm   500 cm   115 cm

....

b) 170 cm   700 cm   100 cm   107 cm   117 cm

....

c) 240 cm   420 cm   204 cm   400 cm   220 cm

....

3 marks

Challenge 3

1 Solve these problems.

a) Maisy has a ball of string. It is 200 cm long. She cuts 40 cm off.

How much string is left on the ball? .... cm

b) Jake is building a fence. It will be 25 m long. He has already built 16 m of the fence.

How much more of the fence does he have to build? .... m

2 marks

2 Work out the following:

a) How many millimetres longer is 11 millimetres than 1 centimetre? .... mm

b) How many centimetres longer is 1 metre than 11 centimetres? .... cm

2 marks

3 Circle the shortest length.

     25 mm $\frac{1}{2}$ m   **2 m**   **10 cm**

1 mark

Total: _____ / 20 marks

☺ **Had a go** ☐   ☺ **Getting there** ☐   ☺ **Got it!** ☐

Mass

Challenge 1

1 Circle the better estimate for each item.

a)

200 g   **20 kg**

b)

1 kg   **50 g**

c)

2 kg   **40 g**

d)

2 kg   **150 g**

4 marks

2 Write the mass shown by each arrow on the scale.

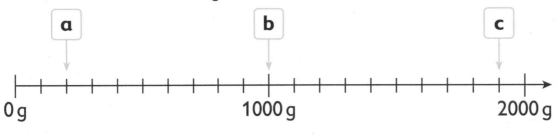

a) .... grams

b) ....kilogram

c) .... grams

3 marks

 Tip   Remember: 1000 grams (g) = 1 kilogram (kg)

3 Read the scale to complete the sentence.

a)

The mass of the bag of sugar is

.... kilogram and .... grams

54

b)  The mass of the bag of rice is

.... kilogram and .... grams

2 marks

Challenge 2

1 Complete these calculations.

a) 250 g + 40 g = [　　　] g

b) 400 g + 75 g = [　　　] g

c) [　　　] = 650 g − 70 g

d) 900 g − 300 g = [　　　] g

4 marks

2 Order these masses from greatest to smallest.

a) 345 g   305 g   505 g   405 g   340 g

....

b) 980 g   809 g   998 g   800 g   900 g

....

2 marks

Challenge 3

1 Solve these problems.

a) Raj buys $\frac{1}{2}$ kilogram of flour and 250 grams of currants.

What is the total mass of the flour
and currants in grams? .... g

b) Nancy buys a one-kilogram bag of sugar and uses 400 grams.

How much sugar is left in the bag? .... g

2 marks

Total: _____ / 17 marks

 Had a go ☐   **Getting there** ☐   **Got it!** ☐

Capacity

Challenge 1

1 Circle the better estimate for each item.

a)

    2 L   **250 ml**

b)

    10 ml   **1 L**

c)

    9 L   **900 ml**

d)

    6 L   **500 ml**

4 marks

2 Read the scale on the beaker to complete the sentence.

a)

There is .... ml of water in the beaker.

b)

There is .... ml of water in the beaker.

c)

There is .... ml of water in the beaker.

d)

There is .... ml of water in the beaker.

4 marks

Challenge 2

1 Complete these calculations.

a) $350\,ml + 20\,ml = \boxed{}\,ml$

b) $\boxed{}\,ml = 705\,ml - 15\,ml$

c) $245\,ml + \boxed{}\,ml = 300\,ml$

d) $\boxed{}\,ml - 20\,ml = 500\,ml$

4 marks

2 Order these capacities from greatest to smallest.

a) 450 ml   405 ml   455 ml   500 ml   415 ml

....

b) 125 ml   250 ml   255 ml   200 ml   150 ml

....

2 marks

Challenge 3

1 Solve these problems.

a) Anji has a litre jar. It contains 400 millilitres of water.

How many more millilitres does Anji need to add
so the jar is full?   ....ml

b) A mug holds 400 millilitres. Peter puts 50 millilitres of milk
into the mug.

How much tea can he pour from the teapot to
fill the mug?   ....ml

2 marks

2 Circle the largest capacity.

$\frac{1}{4}$ litre   **600 millilitres**   **1 litre**   **99 millilitres**

1 mark

3 Yasmin writes three capacities in order, starting with the smallest, but one is missing.

What could the missing capacity be?

$\frac{1}{2}$ litre   .... ml   1 litre

1 mark

Total: _____ / 18 marks

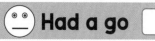 **Had a go**   ☺ **Getting there** ☐    **Got it!** ☐

Perimeter

Perimeter is the total distance around a shape.

Challenge 1

1) Each shape has been drawn on one-centimetre square paper. Find the perimeter of each shape. (Diagrams not drawn to scale)

a)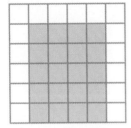

.... cm

b)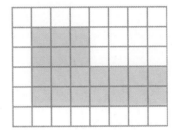

.... cm

c)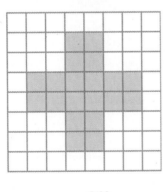

.... cm

d)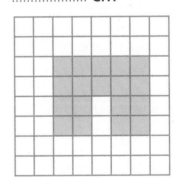

.... cm

4 marks

Challenge 2

1) Calculate the perimeter of each shape. (Diagrams not drawn to scale)

a)

8 cm
8 cm   8 cm
8 cm

.... cm

b)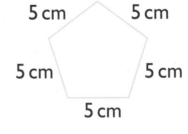

5 cm   5 cm
5 cm   5 cm
5 cm

.... cm

c)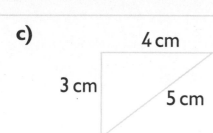

4 cm

3 cm

5 cm

.... cm

d)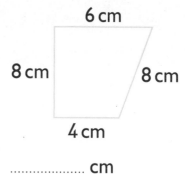

6 cm

8 cm

8 cm

4 cm

.... cm

2 Use this blank space to draw two different shapes with a perimeter of 20 cm. You will need a ruler.

Challenge 3

1 Here are some shapes. Measure the sides and work out the perimeter of each.

a)

Perimeter = ... cm

b)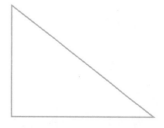

Perimeter = ... cm

c)

Perimeter = ... cm

d)

Perimeter = ... cm

Total: _____ / 14 marks

 Had a go ☐   **Getting there** ☐   😃 **Got it!** ☐

Money

Challenge 1

1 Here is the price list for different fruit smoothies and muffins. Use this to calculate the cost of the items listed.

£1 and 25p   £2 and 50p   £1 and 40p

60p each

a) Kiwi smoothie and chocolate muffin

£ ⬜ and ⬜ p

b) Orange smoothie and blueberry muffin

£ ⬜ and ⬜ p

c) Strawberry smoothie and chocolate chip muffin

£ ⬜ and ⬜ p

d) A box of six muffins (any flavour)

£ ⬜ and ⬜ p

e) All three smoothies (one of each flavour)

£ ⬜ and ⬜ p

f) Two muffins of your choice and an orange smoothie

£ ⬜ and ⬜ p   ⬜

6 marks

Challenge 2

1 The cost of a pen is £1 and 50p.

Calculate the change if you bought the pen from the amount shown in coins or notes.

a)    Change = ⬜ p

b) 🪙🪙🪙🪙   Change = ⬜ p

c) 💷   Change = £ ⬜ and ⬜ p   ⬜

3 marks

2 Here is a table showing the cost of buying tickets for the cinema.

	Adult ticket	Child ticket	Family ticket
Usual price	£8	£5	**£20** for 2 adults and 2 children
Tuesday saver price	£5	£3.50	**£12.50** for 2 adults and 2 children

Use the table to solve these problems.

a) How much will it cost for four children to watch a film on Tuesday?   £ ....

b) How much will it cost five adults to watch a film on a Saturday?   £ ....

c) Two adults and two children watch a film on Tuesday.

How much will they save by buying a family ticket? £ ....

3 marks

Challenge 3

1 Solve these problems. Use £ or p with your answer.

a) Bonny wants to buy a t-shirt for £15 but she only has £14.30

How much more does she need?   ....

b) Dev buys some apples for £1.50 and some oranges for £1.70

How much does he spend?   ....

c)

Jia has these coins. She wants to buy a book for £3.70

Which two other coins would give her the exact amount?

.... and ....

3 marks

Total: _____ / 15 marks

Time

Time facts are important to learn as they help solve time problems.

Challenge 1

1 Complete the facts.

a) 1 hour = ☐ minutes

b) 1 minute = ☐ seconds

c) 1 year = ☐ days

d) 1 leap year = ☐ days ☐ 4 marks

2 Put these words in time order starting with the earliest time in a day.

| noon | evening | morning | midnight | afternoon |

....

.... ☐ 1 mark

Challenge 2

1 Write the time shown on each analogue clock in words.

a)  ....

....

b)  ....

....

c)  ....

....

d)  ....

.... ☐ 4 marks

Teaching Note

Remember, am is morning and pm is afternoon and evening.

2 Write the time shown on each digital clock in words.

a)

06:15 PM

....
....
....

b)

10:55 AM

....
....
....

c)

13:15

....
....
....

d)

21:30

....
....
....

4 marks

Challenge 3

1 Write these lengths of time in order, starting with the shortest.

a)

| 30 seconds | 30 hours | 30 minutes | 30 days |

....

....

b)

| 5 minutes | $\frac{1}{2}$ hour | 120 seconds | 1 hour |

....

....

2 marks

2 Solve these problems.

a) A train leaves at 2:15 pm and arrives $1\frac{1}{2}$ hours later at the next station.

At what time does the train arrive? ....

b) A TV programme starts at half past five. It finishes at quarter past six.

How long did the TV programme last? ....

c) A clock shows 15:02 but the clock is four minutes fast.

What is the correct time? ....

d) Maya's maths lesson starts at 9:25 am and lasts for 1 hour and 10 minutes.

At what time does Maya's maths lesson end? ....

4 marks

Total: _____ / 19 marks

😐 Had a go ☐   🙂 Getting there ☐   😃 Got it! ☐

Mixed measure problems

Challenge 1

1 Find the difference in length between the pencils.

.... ⬜ **1 mark**

2 Shade two different shapes on the one-centimetre grid that have a perimeter of 10 cm.

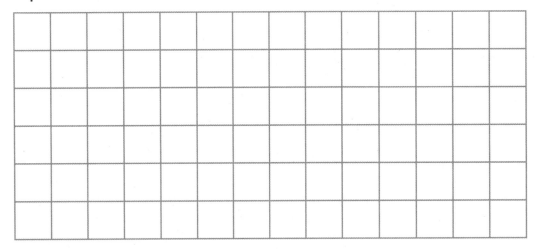

⬜ **2 marks**

3 Tick true or false for each statement.

	True	False
a) June has 30 days.		
b) There are 265 days in one year.		
c) 120 seconds is equal to 2 minutes.		
d) August has 30 days.		
e) December is the last month of the year.		
f) Midday and noon are the same as 12 o'clock.		

⬜ **6 marks**

> **Tip**
> 1 litre is equal to 1000 ml.
> 1 kilogram is equal to 1000 g.

Challenge 2

1 **a)** Circle three items that add together to make one litre.

120 ml   420 ml   550 ml   330 ml

b) Circle three items that add together to make one kilogram.

140 g   250 g   400 g   350 g

2 marks

2 Here are two clocks showing the start and end times of a movie.

Start time   **End time**

Calculate the length of the movie. ☐ hours and ☐ mins

1 mark

Challenge 3

1 Solve these problems.

a) Find the total mass of four bags that each have a mass of 150 g. .... g

b) A plank is 3 m long and is cut into six equal parts. Find the length of each part. .... cm

c) A jug contains one litre of water. Billy pours out 400 ml. How much is left in the jug? .... ml

3 marks

Total: _____ / 15 marks

😐 **Had a go** ☐   🙂 **Getting there** ☐   😃 **Got it!** ☐

Progress test 3

1. Join the numbers to make 800.

   740   140
   660   4
   540   60
   794   200
   600   260
   796   6

   6 marks

2. Each box contains eight stars.

   a) How many stars are there in the three boxes?

   b) How many stars would there be in four boxes?

   c) How many stars would there be in **twice** as many boxes?

   3 marks

3. Here are some numbers:

   745   475   574   547

   Write them in the correct places in the number track.
   The numbers are in order, starting with the smallest.

457			570			747

   4 marks

4. Circle all the numbers with a digit 8 with the value of eight hundreds.

   188   108   810   801   180

   2 marks

5. These shapes all show a fraction shaded green.

   Circle the shape that has the greatest fraction shaded.

   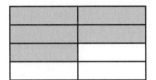 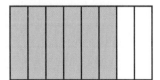 

   1 mark

6. Write the fraction shown by each arrow.

   a)

   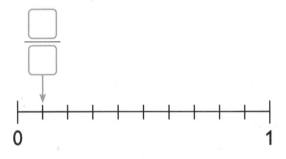

   b)

   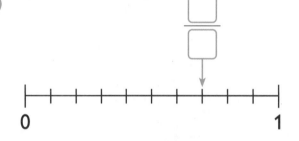

   c)

   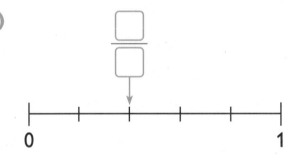

   d)

   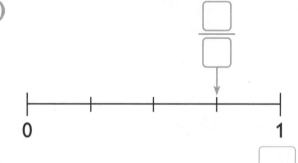

   4 marks

7. Complete the calculations using the bar model.

48					
8	8	8	8	8	8

   a) $\frac{1}{6}$ of 48 = ☐

   b) $\frac{5}{6}$ of 48 = ☐

   c) $\frac{☐}{6}$ of 48 = 48

   d) $\frac{3}{☐}$ of 48 = 24

   e) $\frac{4}{6}$ of ☐ = 32

   f) $\frac{☐}{6}$ of 48 = 16

   6 marks

Progress test 3

8. Shade the bars to complete the equivalent fraction.

$\frac{3}{4} = \frac{\square}{8}$

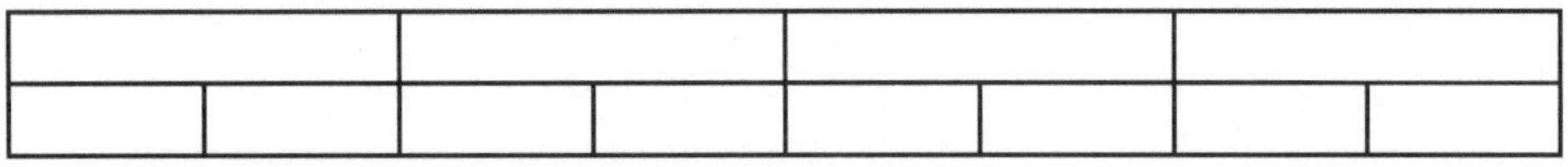

1 mark

9. a) What is the length of the line?

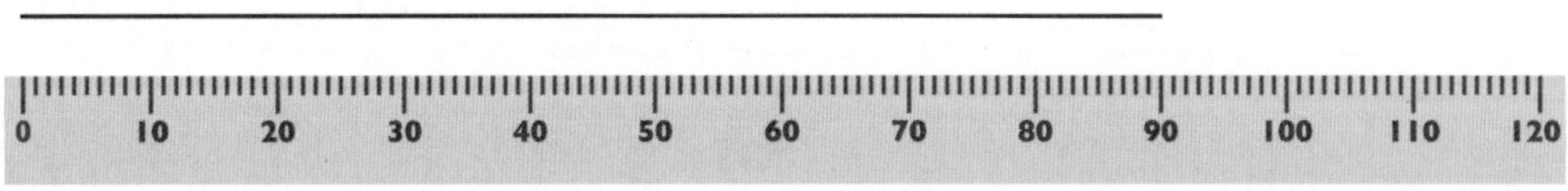

.... mm

b) What is the mass of the bag?

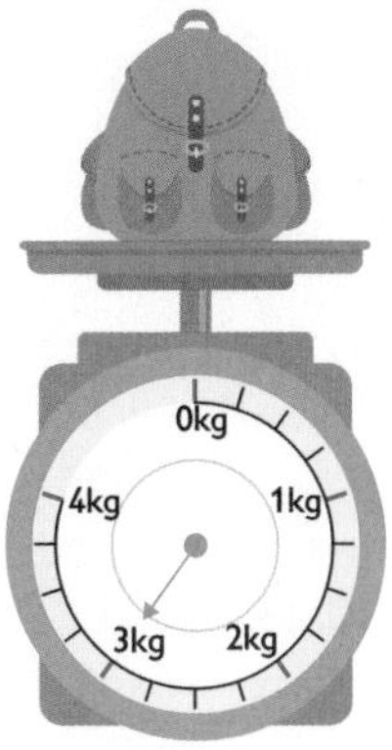

.... kg

c) How much water is in the jar?

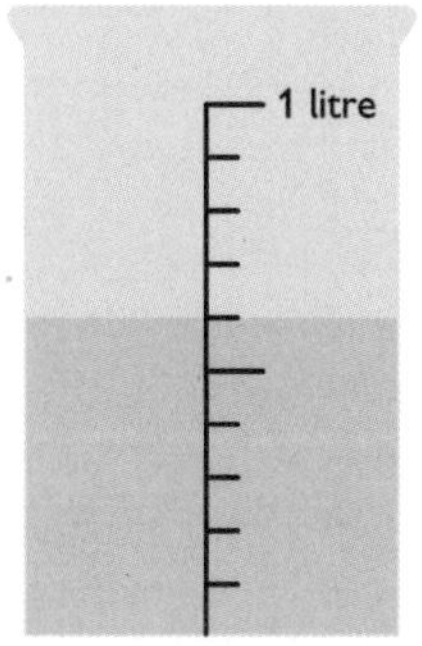

.... ml

3 marks

10. This shape is made from centimetre squares. What is the shape's perimeter?

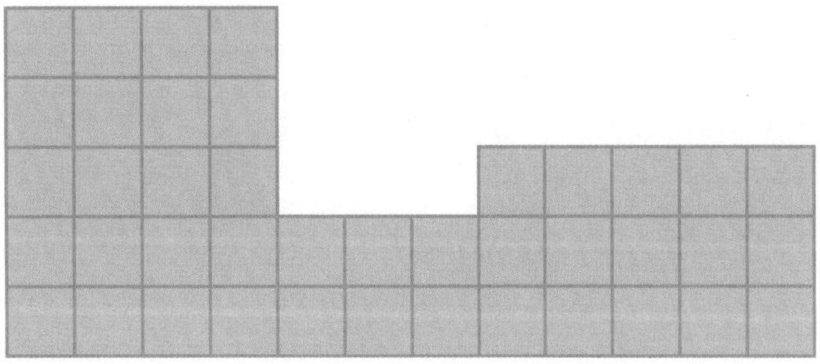

(Diagram not drawn to scale)

....

1 mark

11. Find the missing amounts. Use £ or p with your answers.

a) £1.50 + ☐ = £1.70 **b)** £10.00 – ☐ = £9.50

c) ☐ + 15p = £1 **d)** ☐ – 100p = £1.20

e) £5 + ☐ = £6.50 **f)** £8.60 + ☐ = £10

6 marks

12. Solve these problems.

a) A ball of string is 1 m long. Gemma takes half of the string.

How much string does Gemma have?
Give you answer in centimetres. .... cm

b) James wants to buy a game for £35 but he only has £29.50.

How much more does he need? £ ....

c) A film starts at 5:15 pm and lasts two hours and five minutes.

At what time does the film end? ....

d) A rectangle is 5 cm long and 2 cm wide.

What is the perimeter of the rectangle? ....cm

4 marks

13. Three fractions are written in order, starting with the smallest. One fraction is missing.

Circle the fraction that could be missing.

a) $\frac{7}{12}$ □ $\frac{11}{12}$ $\frac{1}{12}$ $\frac{3}{12}$ $\frac{5}{12}$ $\frac{9}{12}$

b) $\frac{1}{12}$ □ $\frac{1}{4}$ $\frac{1}{3}$ $\frac{1}{20}$ $\frac{1}{10}$ $\frac{1}{2}$

2 marks

14. Order these measures from smallest to greatest.

a) 20 mm   3 cm $\frac{1}{2}$ cm   1 m

....

b) $\frac{1}{2}$ litre   150 ml   900 ml   1 litre

....

2 marks

Total: _____ / 45 marks

Audio test 5

Test Questions

The questions for this test are found on the audio available on the QR code above. Listen to each question and write your answers in the spaces below. Try to answer the questions in the time allowed on the audio.

1. .... ☐ 1 mark

2. .... ☐ 1 mark

3.

```
[pencil on ruler]
0  1  2  3  4  5  6  7  8  9  10  11  12
cm
```
☐ 1 mark

4. .... ☐ 1 mark

5. .... ☐ 1 mark

6. a) .... minutes   b) .... days   ☐ 2 marks

7.

120 ml   550 ml   .... ml

☐ 1 mark

8.

```
[box over box] ↓
0 |—+—+—+—+—+—+—+—+—+—| 1
```
☐ 1 mark

9.   **909 cm**   **990 cm**   **999 cm**   **919 cm**   ☐ 2 marks

10. .... p   ☐ 1 mark

Total: _____ / 12 marks

 Had a go ☐   Getting there ☐   😀 Got it! ☐

70

Audio test 6

The questions for this test are found on the audio available on the QR code above. Listen to each question and write your answers in the spaces below. Try to answer the questions in the time allowed on the audio.

1. 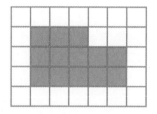 ....

   1 mark

2. **358   308   538   385**

   ....

   1 mark

3. 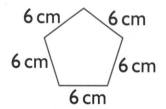 .... cm

   1 mark

4. a) ....   b) ....

   2 marks

5. .... crayons

   1 mark

6. .... p

   1 mark

7. .... m

   1 mark

8. <   >   = $\frac{1}{5}$ ◯ $\frac{1}{8}$

   1 mark

9. a) ....   b) ....

   2 marks

10.   .... cm

    1 mark

    Total: _____ / 12 marks

☺ Had a go ☐   ☺ Getting there ☐   ☺ Got it! ☐

2-D shapes

Challenge 1

1 Complete the table.

Description	Shape Name
A shape with no corners	**a)**
A shape with four equal sides	**b)**
c)	hexagon
A shape with eight sides	**d)**

4 marks

2 Choose the correct shapes in each set.

a) Circle the pentagons.

b) Circle the hexagons.

2 marks

> **Teaching Note**
>
> A line of symmetry can be vertical, horizontal or diagonal. Some shapes can have more than one line of symmetry or none.

Challenge 2

1 Draw all the lines of symmetry on each shape.

a)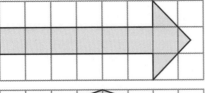

b)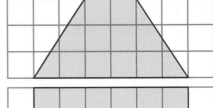

c)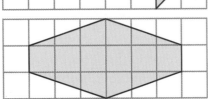

d)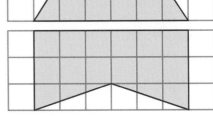

4 marks

2 Write true or false for each statement. Use the pictures to help you.

rectangle   square   pentagon   trapezium

a) A rectangle has two pairs of parallel sides. ....

b) A square has four right angles. ....

c) A regular pentagon has two pairs of parallel sides. ....

d) A trapezium has one pair of parallel sides. ....

4 marks

Challenge 3

1 Here is some squared paper. Draw the shapes.

a) Draw a triangle with a right angle.

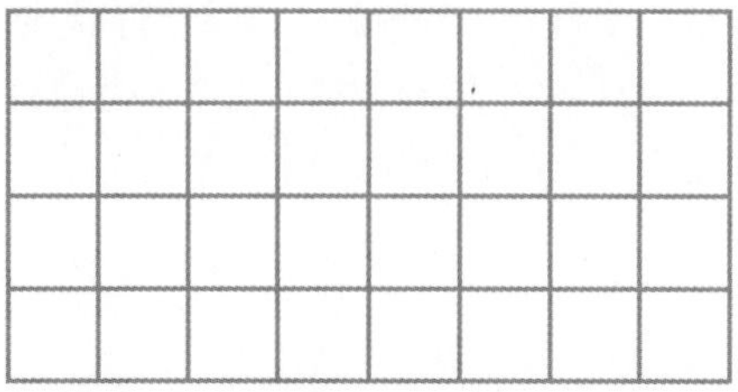

b) Draw a quadrilateral with **no** equal sides.

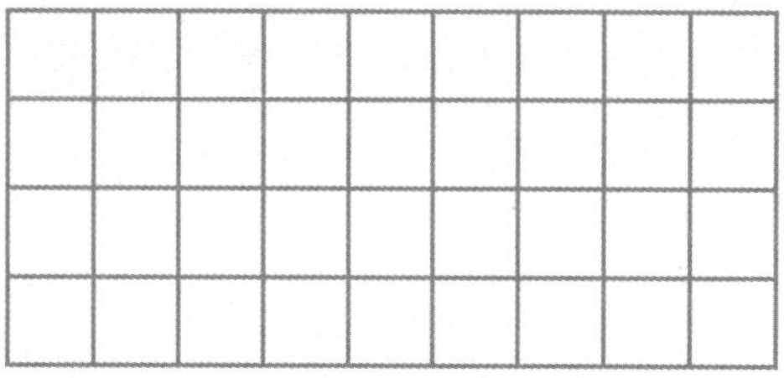

c) Draw a pentagon with **two** equal sides.

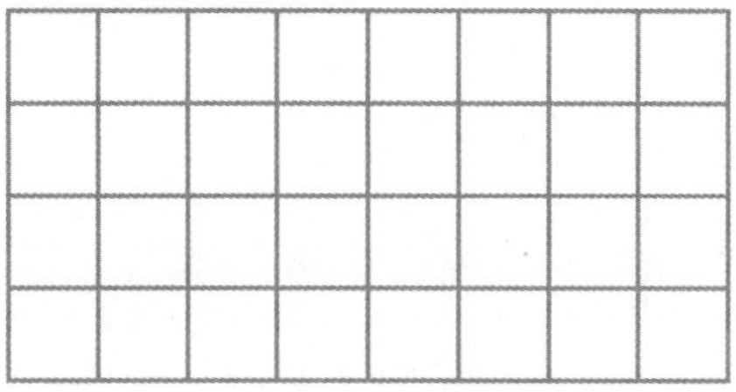

d) Draw a trapezium with **two** right angles.

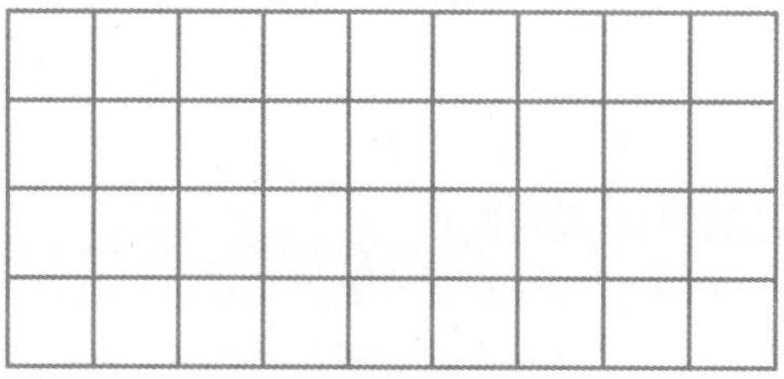

e) Draw a triangle with **two** equal sides.

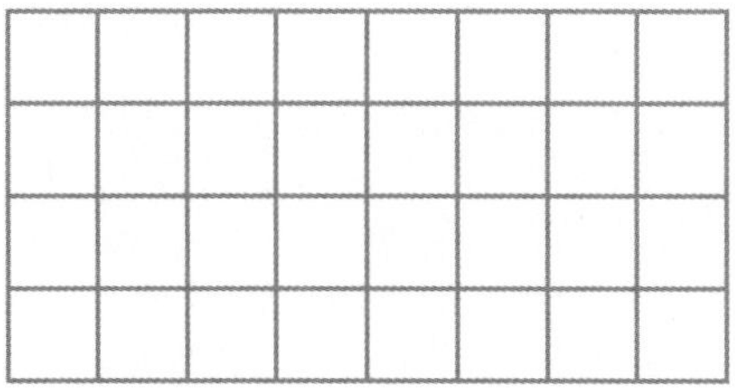

f) Draw a parallelogram.

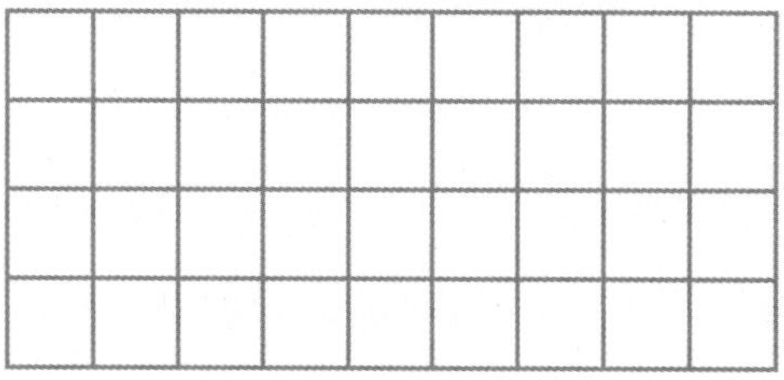

6 marks

Total: _____ / 20 marks

😐 Had a go ☐   🙂 Getting there ☐   😃 Got it! ☐

3-D shapes

1 Match each label to the correct part of the square-based pyramid.

edge   face

base   vertex

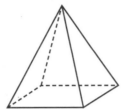

4 marks

2 Complete the table using the 3-D shape pictures to help you.

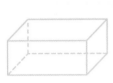   

A   B   C   D

Shape	Name of shape	Number of faces	Number of vertices	Number of edges
A	Cuboid			
B	Tetrahedron			
C	Hexagonal prism			
D	Square-based pyramid			

12 marks

Challenge 2

1 Each set of shapes makes up the faces of a 3-D shape. Write the 3-D shape to match each set.

a)

....

b)

....

c)

....
3 marks

2 Max writes a description of the 3-D shape that he is feeling in a bag. He says: "My shape has vertices and all the faces are flat."

Circle all the possible 3-D shapes it could be.

cuboid   cone   sphere

triangular prism   pyramid

3 marks

Challenge 3

1 Kai has lots of straws and balls of plasticene.

He uses the straws for the edges of shapes and the balls of plasticene for the vertices.

Name the shapes he can make with:

a) 12 straws and 8 balls of plasticene ....

b) 8 straws and 5 balls of plasticene ....

c) 9 straws and 6 balls of plasticene ....

d) 6 straws and 4 balls of plasticene ....

e) Name **two** shapes that Kai will **not** be able to makes using the straws and balls of plasticene.

.... or ....

6 marks

Total: _____ / 28 marks

Turns and angles

Challenge 1

1) Draw a right angle turn on each compass.

   a) North to East    b) South to West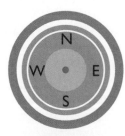

   c) East to South    d) West to North

    4 marks

2) Complete the sentences. Use the clock to help you.

   a) The hour hand moves ☐ right angle/s **clockwise** from 3 o'clock to 6 o'clock.

   b) The hour hand moves ☐ right angle/s **clockwise** from 9 o'clock to 6 o'clock.

   c) The hour hand moves ☐ right angle/s **anti-clockwise** from 3 o'clock to 12 o'clock.

   d) The hour hand moves ☐ right angle/s **anti-clockwise** from 9 o'clock to 3 o'clock.

   ☐ 4 marks

Challenge 2

1) Here are some angles drawn on squared paper.

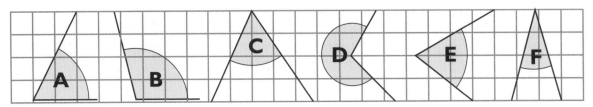

Write the letter of each angle into the correct space in this table.

a) Angles less than a right angle.	
b) Angles greater than a right angle.	

 6 marks

76

2 Sort these shapes into one of the three groups. Write the letter of each shape in the correct place.

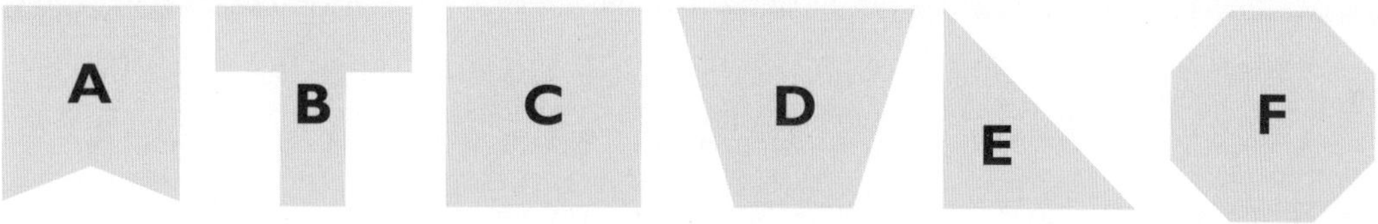

A   B   C   D   E   F

No right angles	1 to 3 right angles	4 to 6 right angles

6 marks

Challenge 3

1 Look at the map.

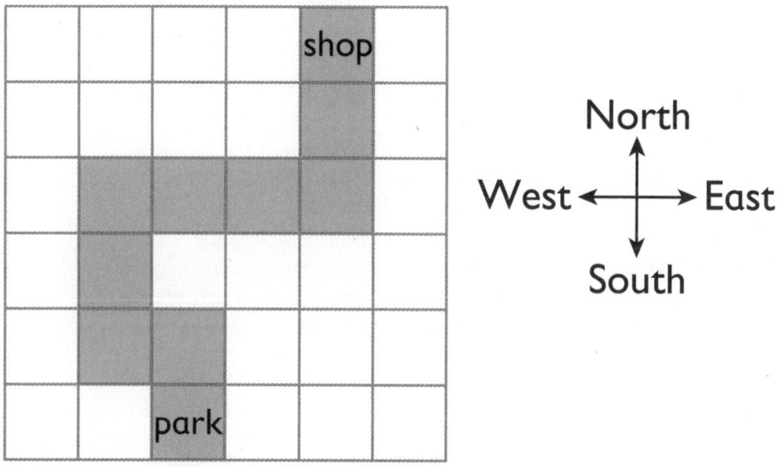

North
West ← → East
South

Mia walks along the shaded path from the park to the shop. Complete the route she walks.

Park, N1, W1, ..., ..., ... Shop

1 mark

2 This is an eight-sided fair spinner.

Where does the pointer move to if it makes:

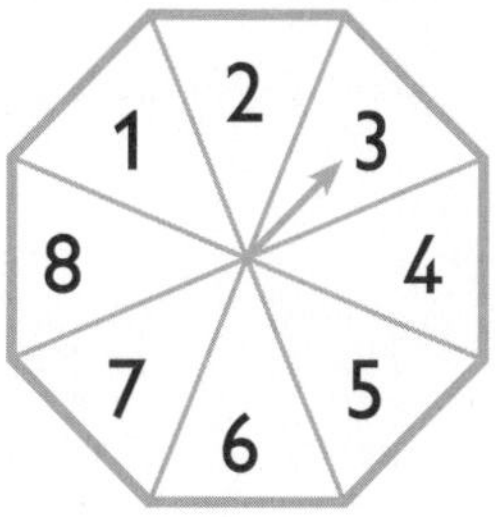

a) a one quarter turn clockwise?

b) a two right angles turn anti-clockwise?

c) a three-quarter turn clockwise?

3 marks

Total: _____ / 24 marks

😐 Had a go ☐   🙂 Getting there ☐   😃 Got it! ☐

Lines

Challenge 1

1 Connect the dots to draw:

a) vertical parallel lines

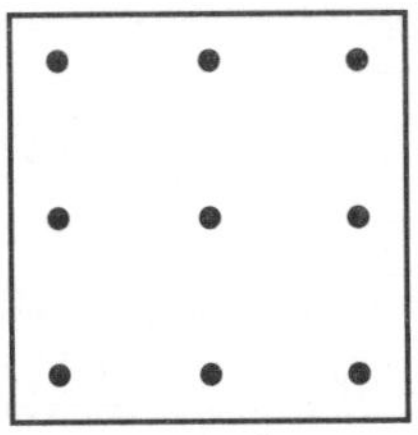

b) horizontal parallel lines

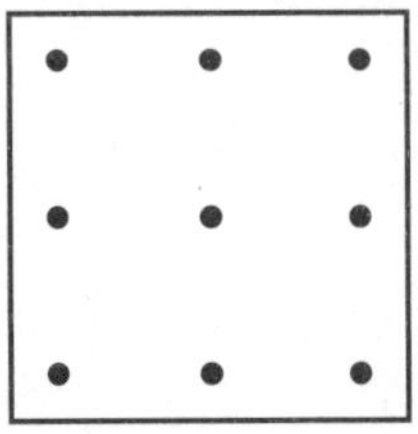

c) perpendicular lines

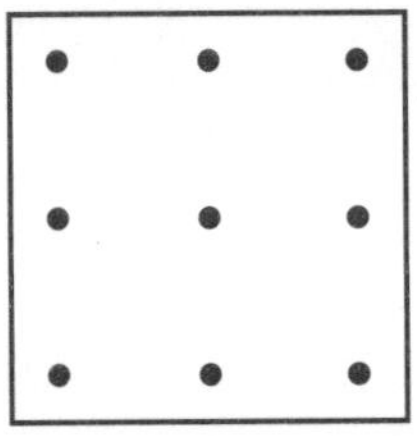

d) different perpendicular lines

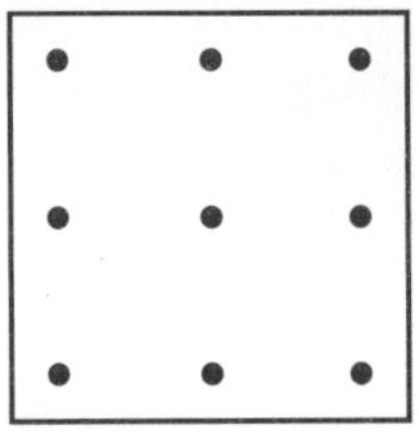

4 marks

2 Circle the pairs of parallel lines.

2 marks

3 Circle the pairs of perpendicular lines.

2 marks

Challenge 2

1 Sort the shapes on the Venn diagram. Check to see if they have parallel sides, perpendicular sides or both. Write the letter of each shape in the correct place.

A   B   C   D   E

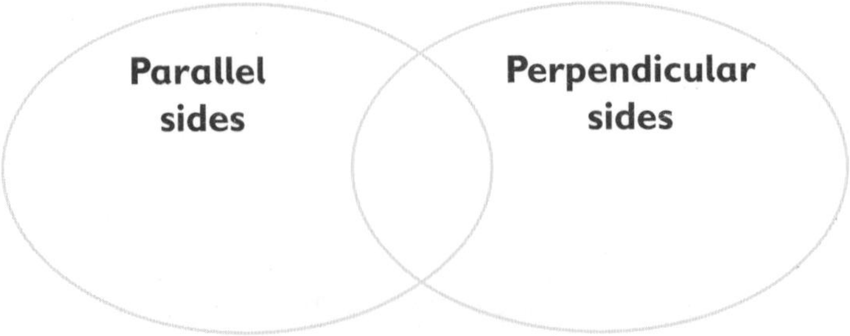

Parallel
sides

Perpendicular
sides

5 marks

Challenge 3

1 Here is a regular hexagon and a regular octagon. Dots have been drawn at each vertex. Join dots to draw a pair of parallel lines.

2 marks

2 Here is another regular hexagon and regular octagon with dots drawn at each vertex. Join dots to draw a pair of perpendicular lines.

2 marks

3 Tick **always true**, **sometimes true** or **never true** for each statement.

	Always true	Sometimes true	Never true
a) A square has two pairs of parallel sides.			
b) A trapezium must have two pairs of parallel sides.			
c) A pentagon does not have perpendicular sides.			

3 marks

4 Here are some letters drawn on squares.

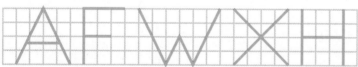

Write each letter into the correct space in this table.

Parallel lines only	
Perpendicular lines only	
Parallel and perpendicular lines	
No parallel or perpendicular lines	

5 marks

Total: _____ / 25 marks

 Had a go ☐   **Getting there** ☐   ☺ **Got it!** ☐

Tables

Challenge 1

1 Here is the weekly school menu.

	Monday	Tuesday	Wednesday	Thursday	Friday
Week 1	Tomato pasta	Vegetable noodles	Tomato pasta	Cheese baked potato	Omelette
Week 2	Baked potato	Tomato pasta	Vegetable pie	Lasagne	Tomato pasta

a) What day in Week 1 is vegetable noodles on the menu? ....

b) What day in Week 2 is vegetable pie on the menu? ....

c) What meal is served on a Friday in Week 1? ....

d) Which meal is repeated the most often? ....

4 marks

2 Here is a table showing the price for four people to go to different theme parks in the UK.

Theme park	Peak time	Off-peak time
Magic Wonderland	£210	£195
Thrill Up	£225	£205
Whirl and Twirl	£180	£150

a) What is the cost to go to Thrill Up at off-peak time?

£ ....

b) What is the cost to go to Magic Wonderland at peak time?

£ ....

c) How much more expensive is it to visit Thrill Up at peak time than off-peak time? £ ....

d) What is the difference in price to go to Magic Wonderland rather than Whirl and Twirl at peak time? £ ....

e) What is the difference in price to go to Thrill Up rather than Magic Wonderland at off-peak time? £ ....

5 marks

Challenge 2

1 Use 24-hour digital time to show that a library is open every week day except Wednesday between half past nine and eleven clock in the morning and then between two clock and quarter to five in the afternoon.

Library Opening Times		
Day of the week	**Morning**	**Afternoon**
Monday		
Tuesday		
Wednesday		
Thursday		
Friday		

1 mark

2 This table shows the number of customers in a café one week. The café is closed on Monday.

Café Customers				
Day of the week	**Morning**	**Afternoon**	**Evening**	**Total**
Tuesday	25	a)	Closed	55
Wednesday	35	40	Closed	b)
Thursday	20	48	Closed	c)
Friday	35	35	d)	100
Saturday	40	50	22	e)
Sunday	55	65	20	f)

Write the missing numbers in the table.

6 marks

Challenge 3

1 Use the table from Challenge 2 to answer these questions.

a) How many customers visited during the mornings, Tuesday to Sunday? ....

b) How many more customers visited on Friday than on Tuesday? ....

c) How many more customers visited on Saturday and Sunday afternoon than on Saturday and Sunday morning? ....

3 marks

Total: _____ / 19 marks

 Had a go ☐   Getting there ☐   🙂 Got it! ☐

81

Bar charts

Challenge 1

1 Use the information from the table below to complete the bar chart.

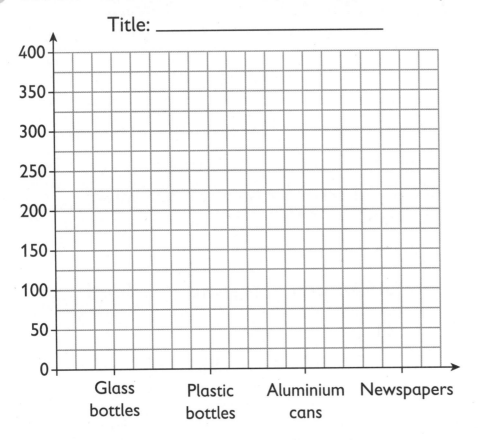

Title: _____

a) Draw a bar for each item using the information in the table.

	Glass bottles	Plastic bottles	Aluminium cans	Newspapers
Number of items recycled	150	300	275	200

b) Write a title on the bar chart.

c) Calculate the total number of recycled items. ....

6 marks

Challenge 2

1 Here is a bar chart showing the different coloured cars that crossed over a bridge on Saturday from 7 am to 7 pm.

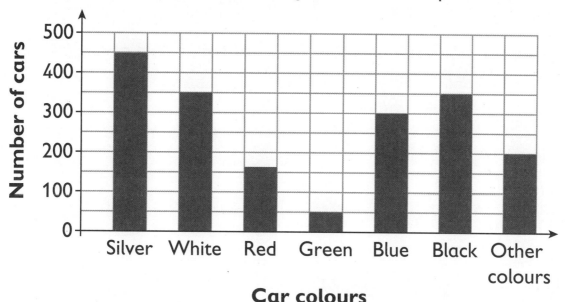

a) What is the most frequent colour car that crossed the bridge? ....

b) How many white cars crossed the bridge? ....

c) Estimate how many red cars crossed the bridge. ....

3 marks

Challenge 3

1 Use the bar chart from Challenge 2 to answer the following questions.

a) What was the total number of silver and white cars that crossed the bridge? ....

b) Calculate the difference between the most frequent colour and least frequent colour. ....

c) From 7 am to 1 pm, 125 blue cars crossed the bridge.

How many blue cars crossed the bridge from 1 pm to 7 pm? ....

3 marks

Total: _____ / 12 marks

 Had a go ☐   Getting there ☐   😃 Got it! ☐

Pictograms

Challenge 1

1 The pictogram shows the number of cups of coffee sold at a coffee shop every day.

 100 cups of coffee

Monday	☕☕
Tuesday	☕
Wednesday	☕☕
Thursday	☕☕☕
Friday	☕☕☕☕
Saturday	☕☕☕☕☕☕☕☕
Sunday	☕☕☕☕☕☕

a) How many cups of coffee were sold on Monday? ....

b) How many more cups of coffee were sold on Friday than on Wednesday? ....

c) Calculate the total number of cups of coffee sold at the weekend. ....

d) How many more cups of coffee need to be sold on Friday to reach 1000 cups being sold? ....

4 marks

2 Use the information to create a pictogram showing the number of marbles each child has.

Tom has 40 marbles   **Jess has 64 marbles**   **Max has 32 marbles**   **Rima has 56 marbles**

◯ = 8 marbles

Tom	
Jess	
Max	
Rima	

4 marks

Challenge 2

1 These pictograms show the number of tents at two different festivals on Day 1.

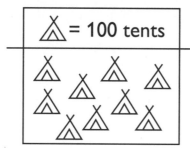

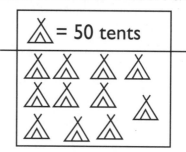

a) How many tents were at the Gloworm Festival? ....

b) How many tents were at the Ecowarrior Festival? ....

c) What is the difference between the number of tents at the Gloworm Festival and the Ecowarrior Festival? ....

3 marks

Challenge 3

1 Use the pictograms from Challenge 2 to complete the following.

a) Each tent at the Ecowarrior Festival had two people.

How many people were at the Ecowarrior Festival? ....

b) At the Gloworm Festival, 200 tents had one person and the rest had two people.

How many people were at the Gloworm Festival? ....

c) The pictogram for Day 2 of the Ecowarrior Festival is:

How many fewer tents are there on Day 2? ....

3 marks

Total: _____ / 14 marks

 Had a go ☐   Getting there ☐   😃 Got it! ☐

1. **Work out the answers mentally.**

   a) $925 + 3 =$ ⬚

   b) $337 + 50 =$ ⬚

   c) $546 -$ ⬚ $= 543$

   d) $758 -$ ⬚ $= 648$

   ⬚ 4 marks

2. **Solve these problems.**

   a) There are eight oranges in a box.

      How many oranges are in four boxes? ....

   b) There are 40 footballers at a tournament.
      There are five players in every team.

      How many teams are at the tournament? ....

   c) A teacher has £50 to spend. She buys 12 books
      that cost £4 each.

      How much money does she have left? ....

   ⬚ 3 marks

3. **Write <, > or = between these calculations to make each
   number statement correct.**

   a) 7×5 ◯ 9×4

   b) $27 \div 3$ ◯ $32 \div 4$

   c) $40 \div 4$ ◯ 5×3

   d) 5×2 ◯ $60 \div 5$

   ⬚ 4 marks

4. **Solve these problems.**

   a) Kev serves 24 cups of coffee. $\frac{3}{4}$ of them have milk.

      How many cups of coffee have milk? ....

   b) Petra is in a race; she must run 12 laps of the track.
      She has run $\frac{1}{3}$ of the laps.

      How many more laps does she have to run? ....

   ⬚ 2 marks

5. **Add these fractions.**

a) $\frac{1}{12} + \frac{4}{12} = \frac{\boxed{}}{\boxed{}}$

b) $\frac{5}{8} + \frac{2}{8} = \frac{\boxed{}}{\boxed{}}$

Subtract these fractions.

c) $\frac{5}{6} - \frac{1}{6} = \frac{\boxed{}}{\boxed{}}$

d) $\frac{9}{9} - \frac{4}{9} = \frac{\boxed{}}{\boxed{}}$

$\boxed{}$ 4 marks

6. **Order these measures from smallest to greatest.**

a)

20 mm	5 cm	3 cm	35 mm

....

b)

1 kg	90 g	200 g	$\frac{1}{2}$ kg

....

c)

50 ml	2000 ml	1 litre	400 ml

....

d)

90 p	£1.50	£0.75	80 p

....

$\boxed{}$ 4 marks

7. **Here are some shapes. Measure the sides and work out the perimeter of each.**

a)

Perimeter = $\boxed{}$ cm

b)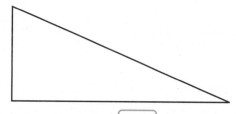

Perimeter = $\boxed{}$ cm

$\boxed{}$ 2 marks

Progress test 4

8. **Here is some squared paper. Draw the shapes.**

   a) Draw a square.

   b) Draw a pentagon with exactly **two** right angles.

   2 marks

9. **Match the shape to the name.**

   a) b) c) d)

   sphere   **pyramid**   **cuboid**   **cone**

   1 mark

10. **Here are four pairs of lines. Circle all the pairs of lines that are parallel.**

    2 marks

11. a) Write the number the arrow will point to if it turns a right angle clockwise.

    b) Write the number the arrow will point to if it makes a $\frac{3}{4}$ turn clockwise.

    2 marks

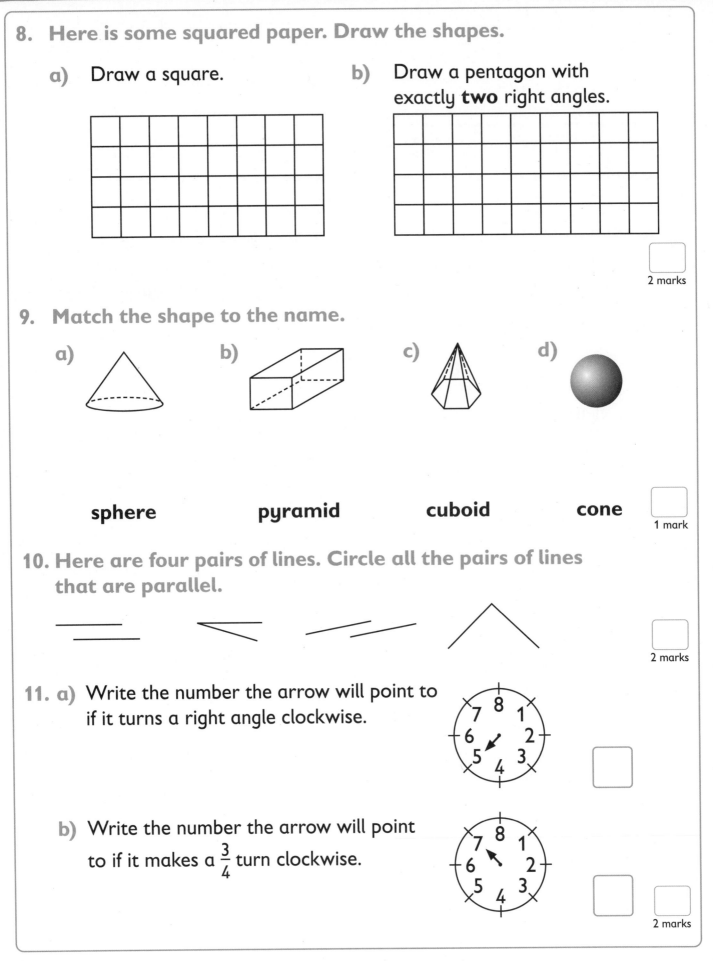

88

12. This table shows the number of children in classes in a school.
One number is missing.

The bar chart is to show the same information.

Class 1	Class 2	Class 3	Class 4
25	30	....	30

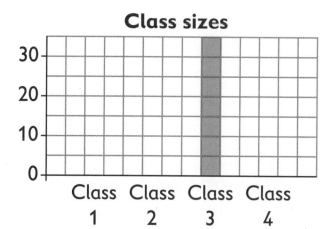

Class sizes

a) Use the information in the bar chart to complete the table.

b) Use the information in the table to complete the bar chart.

c) How many children are in the school?   ....

3 marks

13. This pictogram is used to show 100 exercise books.

How many books are shown by:

a)   ....

b)   ....

2 marks

Total: _____ / 35 marks

The questions for this test are found on the audio available on the QR code above. Listen to each question and write your answers in the spaces below. Try to answer the questions in the time allowed on the audio.

1. ....   [ ] 1 mark

2. .... prizes   [ ] 1 mark

3.
⬆

....   [ ] 1 mark

4.

10 more   10 more

| | 895 | |

[ ] 2 marks

5. ....   [ ] 1 mark

6.

A   B   C   D

[ ] 1 mark

7. .... ml   [ ] 1 mark

8. ....   [ ] 1 mark

9. ....   [ ] 1 mark

Total: _____ / 10 marks

 Had a go [ ]   Getting there [ ]   😃 Got it! [ ]

Audio test 8

The questions for this test are found on the audio available on the QR code above. Listen to each question and write your answers in the spaces below. Try to answer the questions in the time allowed on the audio.

1.  ....

1 mark

2. £ ....

1 mark

3.

a) .... b) .... minutes

2 marks

4. $\dfrac{1}{10} + \dfrac{4}{10} + \dfrac{2}{10} = \dfrac{\square}{\square}$

1 mark

5. .... cm

1 mark

6. ....

1 mark

7. 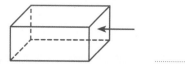 ....

1 mark

8. .... symbols

1 mark

9.

2 marks

Total: _____ / 11 marks

Answers

Pages 6–9

1. a) 16 b) 30 c) 9 d) 15 [4]
2. a) 7 b) 11 [2]
3. a) 17 b) 2 c) 0 d) 18 [4]
4. a) $\frac{2}{4}$ or $\frac{1}{2}$ b) $\frac{3}{4}$ [2]
5. 16 [1]
6. 2nd and 4th shapes circled [1]
7. £2.70 [1] 8. 6 [1]
9. 55, 56, 60, 65 [1]
10. a) 38 b) 82 c) 32 d) 56
    e) 31 f) 13 [6]
11. a) = b) > c) < d) < [4]
12. a) square b) circle [2]
13. a) 80p b) £2 [2]
14. $\frac{1}{2}$ of 10 = 4 [1] 15. 12, 21, 24 [1]
16. a) 30 b) 24 c) 7 d) 9
    e) 10 f) 5 [6]
17. a) 23 b) 10 [2]
18. cylinder and cone circled [2]
19. a) 40 b) 35 [2]
20. a) 5 b) 8 c) 5 [3]
21. 15 [1] 22. 10 kg [1]

Pages 10–11

Challenge 1
1. a) 8, 20, 24, 32 b) 16, 32, 48, 56
   c) 150, 200, 350, 400
   d) 500, 600, 700, 800 [4]
2. a) 4 b) 50 c) 8 (or 4) [3]

Challenge 2
1.

Multiples of 4: 4, 12, 20
Multiples of 8: 8, 16, 32, 64
50 [8]

2. a) 650 b) 30 c) 225 d) 51 [4]

Challenge 3
1. 56 [1]
2. a) Sometimes true (100 is a multiple of 50 and 100, but 150 is a multiple of 50 but not 100)
   b) Always true [2]
3. 8, 24, 48, 64 [1]
4. 100 is not a multiple of 8 [1]

Pages 12–13

Challenge 1
1. a) 295, Two hundred and ninety-five
   b) 353, Three hundred and fifty-three [4]
2. a) 70 b) 800, 70, 6 [4]

Challenge 2
1. a) 5 b) 60 c) 10 d) 0 [4]
2. 106 cm, 116 cm, 160 cm, 166 cm, 176 cm [1]

Challenge 3
1. A = 220 B = 245 C = 280 [3]
2. 245, 422, 524, 552 [4]

Pages 14–15

Challenge 1
1. a) 246 b) 234 [2]
2. a) 314 b) 231 [2]

Challenge 2
1. a) 199 b) 109 c) 89 [3]
2. a) 908 b) 626 c) 608 d) 889
   e) 1000 f) 665 [6]

Challenge 3
1. a) 10 b) 100 c) 100 d) 10
   e) 1 f) 515 [6]
2. 44 [1] 3. 160 [1] 4. 466 [1]

Pages 16–17

Challenge 1
1. a) 135 b) 263
   c) 501 d) 207 [4]
2. a) 209 b) 346 c) 750 d) 645 [4]

Challenge 2
1. a) 593 b) 350 c) 515 d) 621 [4]
2. 300 + 200; 460 + 40; 493 + 7; 399 + 101; 150 + 350; 455 + 45 [6]

Challenge 3
1. a) 75 b) 60 c) 50 d) 185 [4]
2. 565 [1] 3. 645 m [1]

Pages 18–19

Challenge 1
1. a) 212 b) 222
   c) 431 d) 24 [4]
2. a) 712 b) 314 c) 852 d) 182 [4]

Challenge 2
1. a) 339 b) 246 c) 695 d) 298 [4]
2. a) > b) < c) > d) = [4]

Challenge 3
1. a) 3 b) 427 c) 70 d) 784 [4]
2. 876 [1] 3. 122 [1] 4. 9 [1]

Pages 20–21

Challenge 1
1. a) 4 groups of 3, 12 in total
   b) 5 groups of 3, 15 in total
   c) 3 groups of 3, 9 in total [3]
2. a) 3, 9, 21, 27 b) 6, 33, 12, 30
   c) 24, 18, 36, 15 [3]

Challenge 2
1. 3 + 3 + 3 + 3, 4 × 3 and 3 × 4 [3]
2. 9 × 3 → 27 ÷ 3; 4 × 3 → 12 ÷ 3; 7 × 3 → 21 ÷ 3; 5 × 3 → 15 ÷ 3; 10 × 3 → 30 ÷ 3; 2 × 3 → 6 ÷ 3 [6]
3. a) 12 b) 10 c) 24 d) 21 [4]

Challenge 3
1. 18 [1] 2. 11 [1] 3. 45p [1] 4. 9 [1]

Pages 22–23

Challenge 1
1. a) 3 groups of 4, 12 in total
   b) 4 groups of 4, 16 in total
   c) 6 groups of 4, 24 in total [3]

92

2. a) 20, 8, 40, 12   b) 4, 16, 44, 32
   c) 24, 28, 36, 48 [3]

Challenge 2
1. 4 + 4 + 4 + 4, 4 × 4 and 16 ÷ 4 [3]
2. 8 × 4 → 32 ÷ 4; 6 × 4 → 24 ÷ 4; 10 × 4 → 40 ÷ 4; 12 × 4 → 48 ÷ 4; 3 × 4 → 12 ÷ 4; 7 × 4 → 28 ÷ 4 [6]
3. a) 2 b) 8 c) 16 d) 24
   e) 11 f) 5 [6]

Challenge 3
1. 48 **[1]** 2. 8 **[1]** 3. £8.80 **[1]** 4. 32 [1]

Pages 24–25

Challenge 1
1. a) **3** groups of **8, 24** in total
   b) **5** groups of **8, 40** in total
   c) **6** groups of **8, 48** in total [3]
2. a) 16, 88, 56, 32 b) 8, 72, 80, 24
   c) 48, 64, 96, 40 [3]

Challenge 2
1. 9 × 8 → 72 ÷ 8; 6 × 8 → 48 ÷ 8; 12 × 8 → 96 ÷ 8; 4 × 8 → 32 ÷ 8; 8 × 8 → 64 ÷ 8; 7 × 8 → 56 ÷ 8 [6]
2. a) 9 b) 7 c) 24 d) 64
   e) 12 f) 1 [6]

Challenge 3
1. 64 **[1]** 2. 96 **[1]** 3. £64 [1]
4. 2 [1]

Pages 26–29
1. 4, 8, 24, 28, 36 [1]
2. a) 793 b) 400, 60, 2 [4]
3. a) 429 b) 719 c) 741 d) 576 [4]
4. a) 4 b) 15 c) 40 d) 7
   e) 21 [5]
5. a) 75, 255, 725 b) 54, 60, 38 [6]
6. a) 7 b) 30 c) 0 d) 500 [4]
7. a) 230 cm b) 600 g [2]
8. a) 265 b) 718 c) 105 d) 276 [4]
9. a) 484, 504 b) 750, 950 [4]
10. a) 480 b) 520 c) 499 d) 221 [4]
11. a) 925 b) 770 c) 84 d) 780 [4]
12. a) 5 b) 8 c) 60 d) 32
    e) 6 f) 12 [6]
13. a) 110 + 50 b) 5 × 5 c) 60 ÷ 10 [3]
14. 4, 12, 24, 32 [1]
15. A = 160, B = 170, C = 190 **[3]**   16. 123 [1]
17. 90p **[1]**   18. 96 [1]
19. a) 52 b) 14 **[2]**   20. 3 [1]

Page 30
1. 385 **[1]**   2. 650 [1]
3. 28 ÷ 4 **[1]**   4. a) 18 b) 12 [2]
5. 15 and 30 **[2; award no marks if any other numbers are circled]**
6. 412 **[1]** 7. 473 **[1]** 8. 295 **[1]** 9. 200 [1]
10. 784 [1]

Page 31
1. 506 **[1]**   2. 592 **[1]**   3. 100 [1]
4. a) 372 b) 776 **[2]** 5. 420 [1]
6. a) 508 b) 795 **[2]** 7. 6 [1]
8. Accept any multiple of 4 [1]
9. 862 **[1]**   10. 310 [1]

Pages 32–33

Challenge 1
1. a) 80 b) 150 c) 90 d) 160
   e) 240 f) 350 [6]

2. a) 90 (50, 40) b) 42 (30, 12) c) 92 (80, 12)
   d) 124 (120, 4) e) 76 (60, 16) f) 172 (160, 12) [6]

Challenge 2
1. a) 15, 30, 36, 45, 60 b) 20, 40, 48, 60, 80 [10]
2. a) 78 b) 132 c) 305 d) 112
   e) 328 f) 152 [6]

Challenge 3
1. a) £104 b) £112 c) £108 [3]
2. a) 192p b) 220 cm c) 175 kg [3]

Pages 34–35

Challenge 1
1. a) 25, 40, 7, 35, 2, 16
   b) 4, 5, 18, 30, 12, 32, 24, 40 [14]
2. a) > b) = c) > d) < [4]

Challenge 2
1. a) 6 b) 8 [2]
2. a) 72 b) 2 × 4 × 12 = 8 × 12 = 96
   c) 3 × 2 × 15 = 6 × 15 = 90 [9]

Challenge 3
1. a) 4 + 3 × 4 = 80 + 12 = 92
   b) 40 × 3 + 2 × 3 = 120 + 6 = 126 [6]
2. a) 72 kg b) 360p (or £3.60) c) 75 bulbs [3]
3. a) 18 b) 15 c) 13 d) 15 [4]
4. a) 0 b) 2 c) 3 d) 3 [4]
5. 200 [1]

Pages 36–37

Challenge 1
1. a) $\frac{3}{10}$ b) $\frac{1}{10}$ c) $\frac{5}{10}$ d) $\frac{8}{10}$ [4]
2. a) 4 parts shaded b) All parts shaded [2]

Challenge 2
1. a) $\frac{7}{10}$ b) $\frac{3}{10}$ c) $\frac{9}{10}$ d) $\frac{6}{10}$ [4]
2. a) 4.0 b) 2.0 c) 0.8 [3]

Challenge 3
1. $\frac{4}{10}, \frac{6}{10}, \frac{7}{10}, \frac{9}{10}$ [4]
2. a) 3.6 b) 1.8 c) 9.4 [3]
3. a) 2 b) 49 [2]

Pages 38–39

Challenge 1
1. a) 2 b) 3 c) 7 d) 2 [4]
2. a) 4 b) 4 [2]

Challenge 2
1. a) 7 b) 14 c) 4 d) 35
   e) 56 f) 8 [6]

Challenge 3
1. a) £3 b) £3 [2]
2. a) 15 b) 7 c) 18 [3]

Pages 40–41

Challenge 1
1. a) 2 b) 2 c) 1 d) 4
   e) 3 f) 8 [6]

Challenge 2
1. a) False b) True c) True d) False
   e) True f) True [6]
2. a) $\frac{2}{5} = \frac{4}{10}$ b) $\frac{2}{3} = \frac{8}{12}$ [2]

Challenge 3
1. a) < b) = c) > [3]
2. a) Any 3 parts shaded
   b) Any 6 parts shaded

c) Any 4 parts shaded
d) Any 6 parts shaded [4]

3. $\frac{4}{5}$ and $\frac{8}{10}$ circled [1]

Pages 42–43

Challenge 1
1. a) $\frac{3}{4}$ b) $\frac{4}{5}$ [2]
2. a) $\frac{2}{5}$ b) $\frac{3}{6}$ [2]

Challenge 2
1. a) $\frac{4}{8}$ b) $\frac{6}{5}$ c) $\frac{7}{10}$ d) $\frac{6}{7}$
   e) $\frac{1}{6}$ f) $\frac{9}{10}$ [6]
2. a) $\frac{3}{8}$ b) $\frac{2}{6}$ c) $\frac{7}{10}$ d) $\frac{2}{3}$ [4]
3. a) $\frac{5}{8} + \frac{2}{8} = \frac{7}{8}$ b) $\frac{3}{6} + \frac{2}{6} = \frac{5}{6}$ [2]

Challenge 3
1. a) $\frac{8}{8}$ b) $\frac{9}{10}$ c) $\frac{8}{9}$ d) $\frac{10}{12}$ [4]
2. a) $\frac{3}{8}$ b) $\frac{1}{5}$ [2]
3. a) $\frac{2}{6}$ b) $\frac{7}{8}$ c) $\frac{7}{12}$ d) $\frac{4}{12}$ [4]

Pages 44–45

Challenge 1
1. a) smaller   b) greater
   c) greater   d) smaller [4]
2. a) $\frac{3}{5}$ b) $\frac{9}{10}$ c) $\frac{5}{6}$ d) $\frac{3}{4}$ [4]

Challenge 2
1. a) <   b) =   c) >   d) > [4]
2. a) $\frac{4}{5}, \frac{3}{5}, \frac{2}{5}, \frac{1}{5}$ b) $\frac{8}{10}, \frac{6}{10}, \frac{3}{10}, \frac{2}{10}$
   c) $\frac{5}{6}, \frac{4}{6}, \frac{2}{6}, \frac{1}{6}$ d) $\frac{8}{8}, \frac{7}{8}, \frac{5}{8}, \frac{3}{8}$ [4]

Challenge 3
1. a) $\frac{1}{3}, \frac{1}{4}, \frac{1}{5}, \frac{1}{10}$ b) $\frac{1}{6}, \frac{1}{8}, \frac{1}{10}, \frac{1}{12}$ [2]
2. a) $\frac{6}{8}$ b) $\frac{1}{8}$ [2]

Pages 46–49
1. a) 16, 24, 36, 48   b) 24, 40, 64, 72 [8]
2. a) 311   b) 560   c) 439   d) 537 [4]
3. a) 29   b) 36 [2]
4. a) 508   b) 322   c) 475   d) 548 [4]
5. 348 and 841 [2]
6. a) >   b) <   c) >   d) = [4]
7. a) 3   b) 12 [2]
8. a) 3   b) 5 [2]
9. a) greater   b) smaller [2]
10. a) $10 \times 3 = 30$, $7 \times 3 = 21$, $17 \times 3 = 51$
    b) $20 \times 5 = 100$, $7 \times 5 = 35$, $27 \times 5 = 135$ [2]
11. a) $\frac{4}{5}, \frac{3}{5}, \frac{2}{5}, \frac{1}{5}$ b) $\frac{7}{8}, \frac{5}{8}, \frac{3}{8}, \frac{2}{8}$ [2]
12. a) £1.70   b) £2.30   c) £2.80 [3]
13. a) 4   b) 3   c) 5   d) 10 [4]
14. a) 270   b) 225 [2]
15. a) $\frac{4}{5}$ b) $\frac{7}{8}$ [2]   16. a) $\frac{1}{10}$ b) $\frac{2}{6}$ [2]
17. a) <   b) > [2]
18. a) 112   b) 225   c) 87   d) 136 [4]
19. a) 35   b) 25 [2]
20. a) 7   b) 23 [2]

Page 50
1. 125 [1]   2. $\frac{6}{10}$ [1]
3. 56 [1]

4. Accept any fraction equivalent to $\frac{1}{2}$ [1]
5. 50 [1]   6. a) 9   b) 6 [2]
7. 805 [1]   8. 24 [1]
9. $\frac{1}{3}$ [1]   10. a) 32   b) 11 [2]

Page 51
1. 686 [1]   2. $\frac{7}{10}$ [1]
3. < [1]   4. 549 [1]
5. Heaviest: 584 g; Lightest: 408 g [2]
6. 70p [1]
7. a) 4   b) 2.5 [2]   8. 530 [1]
9. 4 [1]   10. $\frac{3}{5}$ [1]

Pages 52–53

Challenge 1
1. a) 19 cm   b) 30 cm   c) 2 m   d) 100 mm [4]
2. a) 6 cm   b) 8 cm [2]

Challenge 2
1. a) 180 cm   b) 380 cm   c) 550 cm
   d) 750 cm   e) 300 cm   f) 800 cm [6]
2. a) 500 cm, 155 cm, 150 cm, 115 cm, 105 cm
   b) 700 cm, 170 cm, 117 cm, 107 cm, 100 cm
   c) 420 cm, 400 cm, 240 cm, 220 cm, 204 cm [3]

Challenge 3
1. a) 160 cm   b) 9 m [2]
2. a) 1 mm   b) 89 cm [2]
3. 25 mm [1]

Pages 54–55

Challenge 1
1. a) 200 g   b) 1 kg
   c) 40 g   d) 2 kg [4]
2. a) 200 grams   b) 1 kilogram
   c) 1900 grams [3]
3. a) 1 kg and 250 g   b) 3 kg and 750 g [2]

Challenge 2
1. a) 290 g   b) 475 g   c) 580 g   d) 600 g [4]
2. a) 505 g, 405 g, 345 g, 340 g, 305 g
   b) 998 g, 980 g, 900 g, 809 g, 800 g [2]

Challenge 3
1. a) 750 g   b) 600 g [2]

Pages 56–57

Challenge 1
1. a) 250 ml   b) 10 ml
   c) 9 L   d) 500 ml [4]
2. a) 4 ml   b) 16 ml   c) 30 ml   d) 90 ml [4]

Challenge 2
1. a) 370 ml   b) 690 ml
   d) 55 ml   f) 520 ml [4]
2. a) 500 ml, 455 ml, 450 ml, 415 ml, 405 ml
   b) 255 ml, 250 ml, 200 ml, 150 ml, 125 ml [2]

Challenge 3
1. a) 600 ml   b) 350 ml [2]
2. 1 litre [1]
3. Accept any number between 501 and 999 ml [1]

Pages 58–59

Challenge 1
1. a) 18 cm   b) 22 cm   c) 24 cm   d) 22 cm [4]

Challenge 2
1. a) 32 cm   b) 25 cm   c) 12 cm   d) 26 cm [4]
2. Two different shapes with a perimeter of 20 cm [2]

Challenge 3

1. a) 14 cm b) 12 cm c) 12 cm d) 11 cm [4]

Pages 60–61
Challenge 1

1. a) £2 and 0p b) £1 and 85p
   c) £3 and 10p d) £3 and 60p
   e) £5 and 15p f) £2 and 45p [6]

Challenge 2

1. a) 50p b) 10p c) £3 and 50p [3]
2. a) £14 b) £40 c) £4.50 [3]

Challenge 3

1. a) 70p b) £3.20 c) £1 and 5p [3]

Pages 62–63
Challenge 1

1. a) 60 b) 60 c) 365 d) 366 [4]
2. morning, noon, afternoon, evening, midnight [1]

Challenge 2

1. a) five minutes past seven
   b) ten minutes to eight
   c) twenty-five minutes past nine
   d) twenty-five minutes to three [4]
2. a) quarter past six in the evening
   b) five minutes to eleven in the morning
   c) quarter past one in the afternoon
   d) half past nine in the evening [4]

Challenge 3

1. a) 30 seconds, 30 minutes, 30 hours, 30 days
   b) 120 seconds, 5 minutes, $\frac{1}{2}$ hour, 1 hour [2]
2. a) 3:45 pm b) 45 minutes
   c) 14:58 d) 10:35 am [4]

Pages 64–65
Challenge 1

1. 4 cm [1]
2. Two different shapes with a perimeter of 10 cm [2]
3. a) True b) False c) True
   d) False e) True f) True [6]

Challenge 2

1. a) 1st, 3rd and 4th items circled
   b) 2nd, 3rd and 4th items circled [2]
2. 2 hours and 20 minutes [1]

Challenge 3

1. a) 600 g b) 50 cm c) 600 ml [3]

Pages 66–69

1. 740 + 60, 660 + 140, 540 + 260, 794 + 6, 600 + 200, 796 + 4 [6]
2. a) 24 b) 32 c) 48 [3]
3. 475, 547, 574, 745 [4]
4. 810 and 801 circled [2]
5. 3rd shape circled [1]
6. a) $\frac{1}{10}$ b) $\frac{7}{10}$ c) $\frac{2}{5}$ d) $\frac{3}{4}$ [4]
7. a) 8 b) 40 c) 6 d) 6
   e) 48 f) 2 [6]
8. $\frac{3}{4} = \frac{6}{8}$ [1]
9. a) 90 mm b) 3 kg c) 600 ml [3]
10. 36 cm [1]
11. a) 20p b) 50p c) 85p
    d) £2.20 e) £1.50 f) £1.40 [6]
12. a) 50 cm b) £5.50 c) 7:20 pm
    d) 14 cm [4]
13. a) $\frac{9}{12}$ b) $\frac{1}{10}$ [2]

14. a) $\frac{1}{2}$ cm, 20 mm, 3 cm, 1 m
    b) 150 ml, $\frac{1}{2}$ litre, 900 ml, 1 litre [2]

Page 70

1. 36 [1] 2. $\frac{5}{6}$ [1]
3. 9 cm [1] 4. 4 [1] 5. 96 [1]
6. a) 60 minutes b) 365 days [2]
7. 670 ml [1] 8. $\frac{8}{10}$ [1]
9. Longest: 999 cm, Shortest: 909 cm [2]
10. 50p [1]

Page 71

1. $\frac{8}{12}$ [1] 2. 308, 358, 385, 538 [1]
3. 16 cm [1] 4. a) 308 b) 285 [2]
5. 9 [1] 6. 80p [1] 7. $3\frac{1}{2}$ m [1] 8. > [1]
9. a) 15 minutes or $\frac{1}{4}$ hour
   b) 5:10 pm or 17:10 or ten(minutes) past five (in the evening) or 10 past 5 [2]
10. 30 cm [1]

Pages 72–73
Challenge 1

1. a) circle b) square or rhombus
   c) a shape with six sides d) octagon [4]
2. a) 2nd and 4th shapes circled
   b) 2nd and 3rd shapes circled [2]

Challenge 2

1. a) b)
   c) d) [4]
2. a) True b) True c) False d) True [4]

Challenge 3

1. Check correct shapes have been drawn. Remember, a triangle is a three-sided polygon with three edges and three vertices; a quadrilateral is a four-sided polygon with four edges and four vertices; a pentagon is a five-sided polygon with five edges and five vertices; a trapezium is a quadrilateral that has exactly one pair of parallel sides and a parallelogram has two pairs of two equal sides and angles. [6]

Pages 74–75
Challenge 1

1. [4]
2. A: 6, 8, 12 B: 4, 4, 6 C: 8, 12, 18
   D: 5, 5, 8 [12]

Challenge 2

1. a) cube b) triangular prism
   c) cylinder [3]
2. cuboid, triangular prism, pyramid [3]

Challenge 3

1. a) cuboid or cube
   b) square-based pyramid
   c) triangular prism
   d) tetrahedron
   e) Accept any two from cylinder, cone or sphere. Also accept any shape with a curved surface. [6]

Pages 76–77

Challenge 1

1. a) b) c) d)
   [4]
2. a) 1 b) 3 c) 1 d) 2 [4]

Challenge 2

1. a) A, C, E, F b) B, D [6]
2. None: D,F; 1 to 3: A, E; 4 to 6: B, C [6]

Challenge 3

1. N2, E3, N2 [1]
2. a) 5 b) 7 c) 1 [3]

Pages 78–79

Challenge 1

1. a) Any two lines drawn from top to bottom b) Any two lines drawn from left to right c) and d) two different right angles created [4]
2. 1st and 3rd pairs of lines circled [2]
3. 1st and 4th pairs of lines circled [2]

Challenge 2

1. Parallel: A, D; Perpendicular: B; Overlap: C, E [5]

Challenge 3

1. Examples: 2. Examples:
   [2] [2]
3. a) Always true b) Never true
   c) Sometimes true [3]
4. Parallel only: W; Perpendicular only: X; Parallel and perpendicular: F, H; No parallel or perpendicular: A [5]

Pages 80–81

Challenge 1

1. a) Tuesday b) Wednesday
   c) Omelette d) Tomato pasta [4]
2. a) £205 b) £210 c) £20 d) £30
   e) £10 [5]

Challenge 2

1. The table should show Closed for Wednesday morning and afternoon; all other mornings should show 09:30–11:00 and all other afternoons should show 14:00–16:45 [1]
2. a) 30 b) 75 c) 68
   d) 30 e) 112 f) 140 [6]

Challenge 3

1. a) 210 b) 45 c) 20 [3]

Pages 82–83

Challenge 1

1. a) and b) See bar chart c) 925
Number of items recycled
   [6]

Challenge 2

1. a) Silver b) 350
   c) Accept any number in the range 160–170 inclusive [3]

Challenge 3

1. a) 800 b) 400 c) 175 [3]

Pages 84–85

Challenge 1

1. a) 200 b) 200 c) 1400 d) 600 [4]
2. Pictogram should show the following number of symbols for each child:
   Tom - 5; Jess - 8; Max - 4; Rima - 7 [4]

Challenge 2

1. a) 900 b) 550 c) 350 [3]

Challenge 3

1. a) 1100 b) 1600 c) 225 [3]

Pages 86–89

1. a) 928 b) 387 c) 3 d) 110 [4]
2. a) 32 b) 8 c) £2 [3]
3. a) < b) > c) < d) < [4]
4. a) 18 b) 8 [2]
5. a) $\frac{5}{12}$ b) $\frac{7}{8}$ c) $\frac{4}{6}$ d) $\frac{5}{9}$ [4]
6. a) 20 mm, 3 cm, 35 mm, 5 cm
   b) 90 g, 200 g, $\frac{1}{2}$ kg, 1 kg
   c) 50 ml, 400 ml, 1 litre, 2000 ml
   d) £0.75, 80 p, 90 p, £1.50 [4]
7. a) 13 cm
   b) Accept any length between 14.5 cm and 15.5 cm inclusive [2]
8. Check correct shapes have been drawn. [2]
9. a) cone b) cuboid
   c) pyramid d) sphere [1]
10. 1st and 3rd pairs of lines circled [2]
11. a) 7 b) 5 [2]
12. a) 35
    b)
Class sizes
    c) 120 children [3]
13. a) 650 b) 475 [2]

Page 90

1. 28 [1] 2. 12 [1]
3. 1 [1] 4. a) 885 b) 905 [2]
5. 200 [1] 6. Shape C circled [1]
7. 750 ml [1]
8. 514 [1] 9. right angle [1]

Page 91

1. 3 [1] 2. £48 [1]
3. a) 10:20 b) 100 minutes [2]
4. $\frac{7}{10}$ [1]
5. 5 cm [1] 6. 10 [1]
7. Face [1] 8. 8 [1]
9. First and fourth options circled [2]